Advance praise for *He Had It Coming*

"Stacy Schneider has created more than just an excellent legal blueprint for women experiencing divorce. *He Had It Coming* is also an invaluable source of tips on nearly every aspect of the process."
—Kathleen A. Miller, author of *Fair Share Divorce for Women, Second Edition: The Definitive Guide to Creating a Winning Solution*

"A great overview to start the divorce process."
—Gayle Rosenwald Smith, author of *What Every Woman Should Know About Divorce and Custody* and *Money: Everything You Need to Know*

HE HAD IT COMING

How to Outsmart Your Husband and Win Your Divorce

Stacy Schneider, Esq.

SIMON SPOTLIGHT ENTERTAINMENT
New York London Toronto Sydney

NOTE TO READERS

This publication contains the opinions and ideas of its author. It is intended to provide helpful and informative material on the subjects addressed in the publication. Please bear in mind that no warranty is made with respect to the accuracy or completeness of the information contained herein, and that relevant laws vary from state to state. The strategies outlined in this book may not be suitable for every individual, and are not guaranteed or warranted to produce any particular results.

This publication is sold with the understanding that neither the author nor publisher is engaged in rendering legal advice or services or any kind of personal professional services in the book. To obtain such advice or services, the reader should consult his or her attorney or other applicable professional.

The author and publisher specifically disclaim all responsibility for any liability, loss or risk, personal or otherwise, which is incurred as a consequence, directly or indirectly, of the use and application of any of the contents of this book.

S|S|E

SIMON SPOTLIGHT ENTERTAINMENT
An imprint of Simon & Schuster
1230 Avenue of the Americas, New York, New York 10020
Copyright © 2008 by Stacy Schneider, Esq.
All rights reserved, including the right of reproduction in whole or in part in any form.
SIMON SPOTLIGHT ENTERTAINMENT and related logo are trademarks of Simon & Schuster, Inc.
Designed by Gabe Levine
Manufactured in the United States of America
First Edition 10 9 8 7 6 5 4 3 2 1
Library of Congress Cataloging-in-Publication Data
Schneider, Stacy.
He had it coming : how to outsmart your husband and win your divorce / by Stacy Schneider.—1st ed.
p. cm.
ISBN-13: 978-1-4169-4935-0
ISBN-10: 1-4169-4935-6
1. Divorce—Law and legislation—United States—Popular works. I. Title.
KF535.Z9S36 2008
346.7301'66—dc22
2007030749

To my superstar sister, Shari Schneider,
for whose invaluable support, love, advice, wisdom,
and generosity I will be forever grateful

Contents

Introduction

Half of all married women in America will inevitably ask:

"What do I do now that my marriage is over?"

Because I was a divorce attorney at the time my own marriage was ending, I knew exactly what to do. I had an arsenal of insider's information to set myself up before the divorce papers were even filed and to ensure my future success on the divorce battlefield. I knew the importance of establishing my own bank account, secretly photocopying our financial records, and staying in the family home while the divorce was under way, no matter how uncomfortable I felt there.

I knew that divorce brings out the worst in people, and that I should keep my "relationship" as amicable as possible, so I could convince my husband to give me what I wanted. I knew to begin working on resolving our issues and dividing our property early in the process, before the divorce became adversarial. I knew it was crucial for me to treat my husband respectfully—or at least appear to—to gain his cooperation and allow for the divorce to move quickly.

Finally, I knew that I could get through my divorce with less agony and frustration if my husband and I communicated without the assistance of lawyers. There have been some divorce situations where I have seen attorney interference do more harm than good, actually causing communicating couples to permanently shut down contact. That is because once lawyers enter the picture, the entire tone of a divorce changes. I have consoled many clients and friends after their so-called "dependable" husbands hired an attorney and reneged on their initial promises to provide for their spouses after the divorce "at the advice of counsel." As an ex-wife and a former divorce lawyer, I want women to know that they can take control of their divorces—sometimes eliminating the lawyers from all or part of the process—and plan stable financial futures for themselves and their children.

What I Learned from My Own Divorce

Almost a decade ago, I walked out of my uncomfortable five-year marriage and straight into divorce court. As an attorney, I already knew the rules of the game and the tricks of the trade. I applied those rules in my own divorce but treated my husband with dignity and respect, without antagonizing him the way a lawyer typically would. After convincing him that we could handle our divorce on our own, without lawyers, I got the exact settlement I wanted with little bickering.

Everyone we knew was shocked at how well my spouse and I got along during the divorce, considering we barely got along during the marriage. When our no-fault divorce was granted by the judge without delay, arguments, or road-blocks, I walked out of divorce court arm in arm with my ex-husband, and we hugged each other good-bye. I have never witnessed a similar sight in all my years of practice. It was at that point that I realized I had a winning formula for a successful divorce outcome that could revolutionize the way women approach the process.

While my experience as an attorney assisted with the paper-work and procedure, the main reason for my divorce success was our ability to eliminate half the battle, most of the nasti-ness, and all of the expense by handling the process ourselves. By negotiating face-to-face without involving lawyers, my husband saved money that went straight to me as part of my divorce settlement. We were able to work together peacefully to resolve all our issues. And although a do-it-yourself divorce is not for everyone, it will always serve you well to understand the process and take control of as many aspects of your divorce as possible.

Taking Control of Your Divorce, with or Without a Lawyer

He Had It Coming will show you which tasks you may be able to perform on your own, without a lawyer, allowing you to shave big bucks off your legal fees. However, this book should not be used as a substitute for legal counsel in cases where professional expertise is necessary or advisable. If ending your marriage involves complicated legal or financial issues, or requires complex litigation or legal argument, professional legal advice will be needed to prevent you from losing out on your fair share. If your divorce is acrimonious or contested, or you have substantial investments or assets, make sure to consult a local attorney. But even with an attorney handling your divorce case, it's always helpful to have a greater understanding of the tasks he or she is performing to demystify the divorce process and allow you to proceed with confidence and control. That's another hidden benefit of having a divorce manual by your side.

Getting Even

For years I have been frustrated that women don't get their fair share in divorce. This inequity exists because most wives are at a natural disadvantage to their husbands when a marriage dissolves, making it harder for them to come out ahead. We typically have fewer resources to help us fight: smaller paychecks, diminished earning potential due to less time in the workforce and more time at home raising kids, and often lack of control over family finances.

So women need to be as strategic as possible when planning their divorces. To help you accomplish this, I will teach you the secret arrangements every wife should make before the divorce papers are filed, as well as the inside tactics, techniques, and maneuvers that divorce attorneys use to gain the upper hand, both inside and outside the courtroom. Armed with information on how to weather the storm, both emotionally and financially, a soon-to-be-ex-wife can survive even the nastiest legal showdown.

A Divorce Road Map

Divorce is a major event in any woman's life. Dealing with the loss of a spouse and family unit, and the change in your identity and standard of living is daunting, particularly when you are in a fragile emotional state. The best thing you can do to take care of yourself is to learn everything you can about divorce before you begin the process, and devise a strategic plan to protect your marital assets and preserve your lifestyle. By arming yourself with a divorce road map, you will help shape the course of your own future, rather than leaving your fate to your soon-to-be-ex or a divorce court judge.

For any wife changing her "I do" to an "I don't," *He Had It Coming* will give you the tactical advantage you need to achieve the settlement you deserve. By being proactive and managing your divorce, you will build the confidence you need to outmaneuver your husband and win. Because where once there was courtship . . . now there's just court.

*   *   *   *

Whether you are contemplating divorce or it's already under way, *He Had It Coming* offers an essential plan to coach you through each stage of the process.

The Ten-Step Plan for Outsmarting Your Husband and Winning Your Divorce

1. Begin maneuvering before your case is filed in court and before you announce to your husband that you are seeking a divorce.
2. Show your spouse that you're in control of the situation by assessing which legal issues don't require a lawyer to resolve and by working on them face-to-face with your spouse.
3. Learn the ins and outs of the legal system.
4. Prepare an ironclad defense and offense.
5. Prepare for potential financial obstacles by collecting documentation of assets, money, and property without alerting your husband.
6. Know what to expect in the upcoming legal battle to maintain your leverage during property settlement negotiations.
7. Think and act strategically. Meet your spouse at the bargaining table with your divorce game plan in place.
8. Apply the negotiation skills and techniques taught in this book to save you money on legal fees.
9. Learn what actions may constitute missteps that can hurt your chances of success in divorce court.
10. Learn how to manage your emotions so they don't interfere with your decision-making abilities.

CHAPTER 1
"I Don't":
When to Re-evaluate Your Lifelong Promise to Your Spouse

We are all familiar with the statistics. Half of all couples who exchange vows will end up in divorce court, and in California the divorce rate is said to be even higher. But no matter how a marriage ends, who's at fault, or who wanted out first, it's still a shock when a husband and wife call it quits.

At the altar, you hope that it will never happen to you. Yet despite best efforts to love and to cherish, to have and to hold, each day in this country yields a fresh new crop of soon-to-be divorcées slugging it out in divorce court. Are you contemplating becoming one of the statistics by changing your "I do" to an "I don't"?

Should I Stay or Should I Go?

If your marriage no longer feels right—or felt uncomfortable from the start—how do you know if you should stay or you should go? The decision-making process is not always clear-cut. Sometimes, even an unhappy relationship can provide emotional support and stability. For some of us, marriage is the only known constant in our lives and a part of our comfort zone. So seeking a divorce may mean trading in security to find quality of life. When we are attached to being "in a relationship," breaking up is hard to do. Consider if your marriage is salvageable or even worth saving. If your husband is unfaithful, destructive, disrespectful, neglectful, engaging in criminal behavior, or excluding you from financial, social, or family decision making, your marriage may be *irretrievably broken*, a divorce catchphrase for "damaged beyond repair."

Signs That Your Marriage May Be "Irretrievably Broken":

- Interacting with your spouse causes you intense stress or anxiety that debilitates you or adversely affects your behavior or emotional state.
- The marriage is a direct cause of your depression, or other physical or emotional illness.
- Your state of unhappiness has reached rock bottom, and you can't remember the last time you weren't miserable.
- You realize your life would be better without him than with him.

Convincing Yourself

Only you—not your therapist, your friends, or your parents— can decide when you are ready to leave your marriage. If you haven't convinced yourself it's time to call it quits, or you just don't feel "ready," then your gut is telling you to hang in there for a while longer. However, if you answer "no" to one or more of the following questions, it may be time to re-evaluate your commitment to your partner.

1. Would I want to continue living my life with a person who could betray me or deceive me or mistreat me?
2. Do I want to continue a marriage where my partner doesn't love me in the way I deserve to be loved?
3. Do I want to be in a marriage where my partner is unwilling to work on our problems or participate further in the marriage?
4. Would I feel satisfied, physically and emotionally, living the rest of my life with someone who wasn't passionate about me or dedicated to growing old with me?
5. Would I feel satisfied living the rest of my life with someone I feel no passion for?
6. Do I want to be in a marriage where I feel emotionally abandoned or abused by the person I love?
7. Would I be fulfilled without sex and physical intimacy in my life, since we seem to be living together like brother and sister, rather than like husband and wife?
8. Do I want to be in a marriage where my husband is so insufficiently committed that he cheated on me?

Avoid Analysis Paralysis

If you think divorce is the right path for you, but you're having trouble initiating it, you may be experiencing "analysis paralysis." This happens when we overanalyze the potential consequences of making a decision to such a degree that we scare ourselves and become paralyzed with inaction. By spending too much time analyzing, we essentially talk ourselves out of taking any steps to move forward or change the status quo.

Many women stay in unhappy or destructive relationships out of fear of what's in store for them as single women back on the market. I suffered through a bad marriage because at one time I irrationally believed that half of something was still something, while half of nothing would leave me with, *well*, nothing. I have friends who are still unhappily attached because they have convinced themselves that they are undesirable or unworthy of a husband who will commit to all the responsibilities a healthy marriage requires.

When evaluating our lives or the question of whether we can make it on our own, women generally seem to be less confident than men. Our insecurity causes many of us to criticize ourselves before we criticize our partners. We doubt whether we are good enough wives. We question if we are pretty enough, witty enough, or supportive enough. We wonder whether we are good homemakers, social planners, and mothers.

The real question we should be asking ourselves is not "Do

we deserve to be with our husbands?" but rather, "Do our husbands deserve to be with us?" Women need to make decisions based on confidence, not fear, especially when contemplating building lives of our own. If you have decided that staying in a loveless, uninspired, or emotionally debilitating relationship will continue to make you miserable, you are doing the right thing by deciding to divorce.

Conquer Your Fear

Another reason women accept being unfulfilled or dissatisfied is because we are afraid of feeling pain. You can overcome analysis paralysis by changing the way you handle your emotions and anxieties. Sometimes fear of pain is more painful than the pain itself. Here's a question for you to answer that can help you take a proactive step: *Which is scarier, staying in a known situation that feels wrong or is toxic (your marriage), or facing an unknown situation (life without your husband) that has the potential to be better than what you are experiencing now?*

Go Guilt Free

You need to be rational and practical when deciding whether to end your marriage. Don't let guilt overshadow your decision making and prevent you from leaving. If your husband's life is a disaster, put aside your guilt over his drinking problem or addictions, his faltering career, his abusive childhood, his unhappiness, or his lack of self-esteem. Don't stay because you don't want to hurt him, or because you think he needs you. Your opportunity to build a new life is more important than allowing him to continue draining your spirit in an unhealthy marriage.

Be Selfish, Not Selfless

Some will say the advice I am about to give sounds cold or callous. After all my years in the courtroom, I say it's just realistic.

Women need to be strategic from the first day they decide they want out.

To exit a marriage, first you must consciously decide to shut the door on your relationship. The second step—which is even more crucial to building your new life—is to begin to think and act "selfishly." If a divorce is going to be the best avenue for you to lead a happier and healthier existence, then it's time to begin focusing on yourself. Start by eliminating your contributions to the relationship. You can no longer play the role of the giving, doting partner. Instead of a wife who is one-half of a marriage partnership, you are now a self-protective sole proprietor. Focus on what it will take to make your life better and how to protect yourself and your kids. Your needs and theirs are now your first priority, and your soon-to-be-ex's needs should no longer factor into your life equation. It's now up to him to look out for himself.

Just Say No to Negativity

Engaging in negative thinking only discourages you from moving forward and sabotages your chance for a new beginning.

Here are some typical negative thoughts that prevent women from divorcing:

"I will never find love again."

"I'll never feel happy or whole again without being married to my husband."

"I don't have the ability to make it on my own."

"My husband is the only man I am capable of attracting. No one else will want me."

By not making changes in your life because you are mired in negativity, you have one guaranteed result: Everything will stay the same. Is that really what you want?

The best way to control negative thinking is to clear it away with positive internal dialogue, what I call "self-talk." Imagine the type of positive support you would give to your best friend if she were expressing similar misgivings to you. Wouldn't you tell her that her self-criticism is inaccurate? That she is being too harsh on herself? That she actually has wonderful qualities and is a good person whom you admire? If so, have the same comforting and supportive dialogue with yourself, and change your negatives to positives. By balancing your thoughts, you will enable yourself to think rationally about this important decision.

So when you start to self-criticize, practice these steps:

Step 1. Stop and step back from your thoughts.

Step 2. Isolate your negative statements in your head so that you can analyze their validity.

Step 3. To analyze without bias, pretend you are addressing your best friend's concerns and providing words of support.

Step 4. Use your "inner voice" to conduct a similar positive dialogue with yourself that contradicts your negative thoughts.

Many of us engage in negative thinking when we are feeling angry, stressed, resentful, ashamed, or insecure. Negative thoughts often straddle the line with irrationality, and they can cloud your judgment and decision-making process. It's important to eliminate negative thinking so you can remain clearheaded and rational when you are weighing the possibility of life without your husband. Once you have made the decision to move forward, it's time to move ahead with the Pre-Divorce Plan.

CHAPTER 2
The Pre-Divorce Plan: The Secret Steps Every Wife Should Take Before the Divorce Papers Are Filed

Men often have the advantage in divorce. That's because the spouse with greater financial resources usually walks away with more money. Also, the results of a divorce often send stay-at-home moms and nonworking wives back to the workforce with little experience and/or outdated job skills. The best way for women to improve their chances for success is to begin strategizing before serving their husbands with papers. Prepare for your divorce and protect yourself financially by following my ten-step Pre-Divorce Plan. I took years to devise the plan for my female divorce clients and am happy to share it with you. I know it works, because I used it myself during my own divorce.

The plan outlines the crucial tasks you must complete, and the resources you should gather before the divorce papers are filed, to give you the tactical advantage you need. The key to implementing the plan is to keep your husband in the dark that you intend to end the marriage. This way you can complete the steps without attracting his attention, and place yourself in the best position—financially, strategically, and emotionally—to proceed with the upcoming legal battle. It is best to implement the plan at least six months before you file for divorce, but if you have been or are about to be served with papers, start the plan immediately for the best results.

The Ten-Step Pre-Divorce Plan: Protecting Yourself Before the Storm Hits

Step 1: Investigate Family Finances and Debts

Use this time to arm yourself with the facts about your family finances. Educate yourself on household income and debt by reviewing bills, loan documents, your husband's pay stubs, bank account statements, brokerage account statements, and by speaking with the family accountant.

In many marriages, when the wife doesn't work or earns less than her spouse, she is left out of the loop when it comes to family financial planning, investment decisions, and money management. If you have been kept in the dark about finances, if your husband pays all the bills or handles all the money, or if you believe he's capable of hiding assets from you, it's time to investigate and educate yourself very quickly on how your household runs. By doing your homework before the divorce begins, you will know what should be yours when it's time to walk away.

STEP 2: APPLY FOR YOUR OWN CREDIT CARD

Prepare for the possibility that once the divorce is announced, your husband might cancel your credit cards or remove you as an additional cardholder on his account. Apply for your own credit card pre-divorce if you don't already have one. Should you wait until you are single, credit card companies may deny you an individual card or only qualify you for a card with exorbitant interest rates.

Women are more likely to qualify for cards when they are married, because creditors allow wives to benefit from joint marital credit. Joint credit is based on the combined assets of both spouses. Many creditors will award credit to a wife with no credit or poor individual credit by relying on the husband's credit. The theory is that marital credit provides lenders with a reliable safety net to cover debts should you default, since they can seek repayment from two parties instead of one. Put this theory to use: Apply for a credit card while you still have joint marital credit, thereby creating your own safety net.

STEP 3: ESTABLISH A CREDIT HISTORY

Next, take some time to establish your own credit history as soon as possible. A credit history shows future lenders that you are a good risk to receive loans or lines of credit. This financial track record of debt repayment is used to qualify you for bank loans, business loans, mortgages, credit cards, or even to rent an apartment.

Married women often have limited credit histories when their husbands handle the family finances exclusively and/or exclude their wives' names from mortgages or loan applications. If post-divorce you need a bank loan to start a business or buy a home and your credit history is limited to sharing a joint credit card with your husband, it probably won't be enough to convince potential lenders that you will be a reliable borrower. That is why it is crucial to establish a credit history while you are still married and have joint financial resources available.

To work toward this goal, take out a small bank loan where you are the sole borrower, and then pay it off rapidly. If you own a home, secure a small home equity loan in your name alone and complete all the payments over the next few months. (You must be one of the titleholders to the property to qualify for the loan.) The small amount of money you will lose in interest and fees is nothing compared to the benefits of the credit you are building for your future.

Be Careful: Make sure the debt you choose to acquire for the purpose of building credit isn't overwhelming. By attaching your name to an unmanageable loan, you risk defaulting or ruining your credit.

Step 4: Open Your Own Bank Account

Once the divorce begins, you will need your own money for living expenses, bills, court fees, or hiring a lawyer. Plus, you never know what hardship is going to present itself before or during the process. Either spouse can request for a bank to freeze joint accounts while a divorce is pending, preventing both parties from withdrawing money. Your husband can cut off your credit cards or cash supply. Having your own bank account will help you stay afloat until you receive a settlement, an alimony check, or an award for attorney's fees.

Open an individual bank account before you file for divorce if you don't already have one. If you have a joint account with your husband, remove half of the funds and put them in your individual account so he will have no access once the court action begins. (The best time to do this is just before you file your divorce papers, to ensure that you don't tip your husband off too early.) Few divorce courts will criticize this move, because it is presumed under the law that each of you owns the contents of a joint account equally.

Be Careful: Don't be greedy! If you take more than your share of the joint account before you file for divorce, you are helping yourself to extra money that does not belong to you. A judge can view this action as improper **self-help** (helping yourself while hurting your husband) and punish you during the divorce proceedings. See Chapter 9 for the consequences of improper divorce conduct.

Your individual bank account will also enable you to protect your assets if your husband suddenly stops making the payments on loans for marital property, like a home or a car. It happened to one wife, whose deceptive husband hatched a dirty plan. He stopped paying the mortgage on the couple's home after they separated, planning to let it go into foreclosure. His plan was to have his best friend buy the house back from the bank at a reduced price, and then convey it back to him once the divorce was final. Fortunately, the wife caught on to the scheme early. By using funds from her individual bank account, she was able to hold on to the house by making the payments herself, during the time it required for her to get a divorce court judge to intervene on her behalf. The court eventually forced the husband to continue making mortgage payments until it was decided how the house would be divided.

Extra Attention Required: If your husband stops making mortgage payments and he is financially able to do so, you have the option of asking the divorce court judge to order him to continue paying. A lawyer can assist you in filing a written motion for the court to intervene. But if your husband legitimately claims he has no money, the court may not be able to help. You will still need your own resources to temporarily cover expenses.

STEP 5: ACCUMULATE A CASH RESERVE

Start now to accumulate a cash supply of your own, well before the divorce papers are filed. You don't want to end up strapped for money or unable to meet your daily living expenses when the legal action begins. Although you may have the option of seeking an emergency court order for your husband to pay *temporary support* (alimony awarded while the divorce is pending, but subject to change once the divorce is final), you might not have the opportunity to see a judge quickly enough to meet your needs. Requests for court orders must be filed in writing. It can take several weeks for your request to be scheduled on the court calendar, and then for a judge to review and decide if it will be granted.

Every little bit helps to build up a cushion to help you get through the tight spots, so be creative. Here are some practical tips to help you grow a cash reserve:

Bank your paycheck

- If you are employed, begin banking as much of your salary as possible in your individual account. You can do this if it's possible to spend only his money on household expenses and bills.

Be Careful: In community property states (such as Arizona, California, Idaho, Louisiana, Nevada, New Mexico, Texas, Washington, and Wisconsin) your husband may be entitled to half your salary earned during the marriage. He may later make a claim for part of the earnings you deposited into your own account. So don't spend all of this type of savings if you can help it, in case you need to reimburse him for his share.

Bargain shop and pocket the difference

- If you are a stay-at-home mom and use his salary to cover household expenses, shop smart and keep what you save for yourself. Buy what's on sale at the supermarket, shop for household supplies at discount retailers or warehouses, or skimp on purchases, and keep the change for yourself. Your husband doesn't need to know the details when you pocket the benefits of your bargains!

Sell, sell, sell

- If money's tight or you have no household allowance, another way to raise cash is to sell your personal property. Sell your old clothes or spare junk from your garage to thrift stores, antique shops, or consignment shops.

Bonus Tip: Sometimes you don't have as much time to plan in advance. Here's what you can do in little or no time to raise some extra cash:
    * Post a free sales advertisement online at www.craigslist.org.
    * Hold a garage sale or eBay auction.
You won't get rich from your endeavors, but you *can* pocket a decent chunk of change from a weekend's worth of work.

STEP 6: OPEN YOUR OWN SAFE-DEPOSIT BOX

Remove your important documents (particularly those you'll need in the divorce) and your valuables from the house. Place them in your own safe-deposit box so that you avoid the risk of them being misplaced or the possibility of your husband taking them after the divorce papers are filed.

STEP 7: GET A POST OFFICE BOX AND A NEW PRIVATE E-MAIL ACCOUNT

To keep important documents private, begin rerouting personal mail like accountant's bills, private correspondence, and individual credit card statements away from your husband and your home. Open your own post office box.

Have personal e-mails and potential divorce-related communications sent to a new private e-mail account or address that your husband can't access.

Bonus Tip: If you decide to move out or rent an apartment when you separate, a post office box will also help keep your new address private from your husband and prevent him from dropping by uninvited.

STEP 8: SEARCH FOR ASSETS AND PHOTOCOPY FINANCIAL DOCUMENTS

Prepare for your divorce by searching for documents that determine the value of your joint property, personal property, savings, income, marital assets, and your husband's net worth. You don't need to hire a private investigator. All you need is a photocopier. Make copies of all family financial documents that you collect to use as "evidence" for your upcoming divorce.

Such documents include: money market and bank account statements, mutual funds, stock certificates, bonds, employment and retirement benefit statements, life insurance policies, and deeds to property. (Chapter 3 provides specific instructions and insider tips on where to search for money, property, and proof of assets.) By collecting financial documentation, you can prevent your husband from cheating you out of your share when marital property gets divided.

If you don't act early, when household documents are within your reach, information can suddenly "disappear" once the divorce begins. An asset search is one of the most important tasks you can accomplish pre-divorce, because your husband may cut off your access to valuable divorce ammunition by locking you out of the safe, cleaning out the bank accounts, hiding his checkbook, or removing everything from the house if he moves out once the legal action begins.

Keep your photocopies in a safe place, such as your personal safe-deposit box (see Step 6) or with a family member, until you will need them for the divorce action.

Financial Document Search Checklist

❏ **Bank Accounts, Financial Accounts, and Financial Instruments**

Gather the account numbers and institutional statements from all money market accounts, bank accounts, mutual funds, stock certificates, bonds, and any other financial holdings or accounts you can find.

❏ **Credit Card Statements**

Review all household credit card statements to see how much he has been spending and where the money has been going.

❏ **Retirement Benefits**

Get account numbers and statements for 401(k) plans, IRAs, and other retirement benefit accounts.

❏ **Mortgage Statements**

If you own a home, get a copy of the statement for the mortgage or any other type of homeowner loan, such as a home equity loan or home equity line of credit.

❏ **Life Insurance Policies**

Obtain the policy numbers of any life insurance policies. Copy the declarations pages, which "declare" or spell out the terms.

❏ **Employment Benefits**

Try to locate paperwork indicating whether your husband has an employee profit-sharing plan or stock option plan, or if he has a bonus schedule.

❏ **Appraisals**

Collect and photocopy any certificates of appraisal for jewelry, art, antiques, and other valuable property.

❏ **Proof of Ownership Documents**

Photocopy property deeds for land or housing, and certificates of title for cars or boats.

❏ **Wills and Trusts**

Locate a copy of your and your husband's last will and testament, as well as trust instruments. Wills and trusts often reference the existence of a spouse's property or possessions. If you and he previously executed joint wills at a lawyer's office, they may be on file there. Request that a copy be mailed to you. (If your husband executed an individual will, you won't have access to it without his authorization due to confidentiality rules.)

> **Bonus Tip:** You may want to pick up a copy of your will in person or have the document sent to your personal post office box, so that your husband doesn't see a lawyer's return address in your mail pile and get suspicious.

❏ **Income Tax Returns**

Contact your accountant and ask for copies of your joint tax returns going back five years. (If you and your spouse filed individually, the usual way to obtain your husband's separate returns is by subpoena or a legal document request after the divorce lawsuit begins.) Returns may prove to be valuable evidence during your divorce, especially if your husband tries to undervalue his net worth, lies about his income or holdings, or hides assets.

❏ **Pay stubs and W-2s**

Collect as many of your and your spouse's recent pay stubs or W-2 statements of earnings that you can find.

STEP 9: INVENTORY YOUR PROPERTY

After you have educated yourself on family finances and located marital assets, inventory your property and debts. Create an asset and debt inventory checklist establishing what property and obligations will need to be divided. Your inventory list should be broken down into three areas: personal property, real estate, and debts.

Personal Property Inventory

Make a list of tangible personal property (any property that you can "touch") owned by you and your husband that's worth more than five hundred dollars. Assign a dollar value to each item. Make sure to include: antiques, jewelry, art, cars, collectibles, equipment, boats, furniture, and any other items that will need to be divided.

This list will also help you keep track of your possessions in case your husband tries to sneak marital property out the door during the divorce.

Real Estate Inventory

List any real estate you own and determine if the property is titled to you, your husband, or both.

How real estate is divided often depends on its value. Have your property appraised or research sale prices of similar listings in your neighborhood so you will have an idea of its worth ahead of time. A website that offers comparable property values in your area is www.trulia.com.

Debt Inventory

Identify and determine the value of all outstanding debts, including but not limited to: car loans, home mortgages and home equity loans, commercial mortgages on business or rental property, business and school loans, and credit card debt. Keep a list of loan account numbers, whose name the debt is in, names and addresses of creditors, and whether the debt was acquired before or after the marriage. This will come in handy later when you and your spouse decide who will take responsibility for marital debt. Your debt list will also help you track what your husband owes to creditors, so you can insulate yourself from liability for his debts after the divorce.

Sample Property Inventory List

Personal Property	*Debt*
Cartier watch	Mortgage: $1,600/mo
Nissan	($50,000 owed)
Honda	Visa: $5,000 owed
Antique grandfather clock	Mastercard: $1,000 owed
Plasma TV	Condo fees: $300/mo
Oil painting	(2 months behind, $600 owed)
Persian rug	Nissan lease: $375/mo
Motorbike	($4,500 owed)
Pool table	
Home computers	
Sterling silver platter	

Real Property

Condo (joint value approximately $250,000)

Time share (value approximately $5,000)

Step 10: Take Photographs of Possessions and Find Receipts

In a divorce, valuable items often mysteriously turn up "missing." Create a visual record of what you own by taking photographs of your property. This way, if your spouse starts hiding or selling marital property or possessions, photographic documentation will help you fight back by providing proof of what was once there.

Photographs can also add credibility to your request for a higher financial award. When your goal is to get the best possible property division results, there is a big difference between telling the judge about your marriage lifestyle and showing him. Come to court prepared with photos showcasing your car, home, furnishings, artwork, antiques, vacations or vacation rentals, valuables, or even landscaping. You may increase your chances of convincing the judge to give you a higher share of the marital assets.

Next, collect any receipts you can from big-ticket purchases. These will provide proof of the property's value and its existence.

****

Take It from Someone Who Knows: A friend of mine came home from work one night and was served with divorce papers on his front doorstep. When he entered his house, his wife was gone, along with the televisions, computer, dining room table and chairs, couch, lamps, and just about everything else they owned, down to the silverware. The only items left were his clothes hanging in the closet.

At first he thought he had been robbed. And in essence, he had been. His wife took advantage of him at a time he didn't suspect the marriage was in trouble, and "stole" all the furniture. If he had kept receipts from expensive purchases, he would have had an easier time proving to the court that those items existed before they had vanished. Instead, it took a costly court battle to re-create the value of his missing property for the judge.

****

Implementing the Pre-Divorce Plan is the most important task you can accomplish to ensure financial stability and a successful divorce outcome. I tailored the plan specifically for women to help empower them for the legal battle ahead. I followed the same guidelines to prepare for my own divorce. It turned out to be the best investment of time and effort I ever made.

To stay organized and efficient, here's a review checklist for you to make sure you complete all the steps.

The Pre-Divorce Plan Checklist

□ Investigate family finances and debts.

□ Apply for your own credit card.

□ Establish a credit history.

□ Open your own bank account.

□ Accumulate a cash reserve.

□ Open your own safe-deposit box.

□ Get a post office box and a new private e-mail account.

□ Search for assets and photocopy financial documents.

□ Make a property inventory checklist.

□ Take photos of possessions and find receipts.

CHAPTER 3

Show Me the Money! Where to Find the Dollars, Tangibles, and Assets of Your Marriage

You are entitled to an overview of your marital financial status and to review any documents referencing marital income, assets, and debt. To obtain this "full picture," it's essential to start investigating and substantiating what funds exist as a result of your marriage partnership. When I was planning for my divorce, I went into my husband's home office when he was at work and gathered every document I could find. There was so much paper in his desk and on his bookshelves that I had to draw myself a map of where I found everything, so I could return each item to its proper place without arousing his suspicion that I was combing through his file folders.

I rushed to the copy store and duplicated everything he had. I ended up with a three-inch-thick stack of paper detailing credit card spending I was unaware of, tens of thousands of dollars in bonuses from his employer that never made it into our joint account, and retirement account savings I never knew existed. You can be sure this information was very useful to me to increase the value of my property settlement award.

There's a natural inclination to feel guilty for looking through your husband's desk drawers or filing cabinet as if you're peeking into his personal property. But you should remember that that mind-set is a trap. What you're looking for is marital money and assets—things that are in part yours—and knowing about them will increase your odds of winning a fair divorce settlement. With your full financial picture exposed, you can prevent your spouse from paying you less than he really should when it's time to divide your property. Here's where to look for evidence.

Your Home

The home office, desk drawer, and home safe are invaluable sources of information for your divorce. When your husband's not there, go through the family paperwork and photocopy all the financial documents you can find. Learn where all accounts are located and where statements are kept.

Safe-Deposit Box

If you have access, examine what your husband keeps in the safe-deposit box. Many people store important documents or valuable possessions there, such as savings bonds, property deeds, income tax records, loan documents, stock certificates, or jewelry. If your signature does not authorize access to the box, you will need to obtain a court order once the divorce begins, to impound the box and inventory its contents.

The Computer

An excellent source of information about your marriage is usually contained inside your husband's personal computer. You can check his e-mails, the history of his Internet search queries, and any files or information he has downloaded onto his hard drive.

Am I promoting invasion of his personal space to gather useful information for your divorce? Yes, but only so long as you do not invade his legal privacy.

You are not entitled to view files that are password protected. No matter how tempted you are to crack his password code, review only screens where your husband hasn't taken steps to prevent outside access. Hacking into his computer or forcing your way into protected areas may constitute an invasion of privacy, a form of eavesdropping, or an illegal interception, and may land you in serious trouble, even exposing you to criminal liability.

Also, there are many states where the use of *spyware* (programs that secretly collect the information stored on a computer and transfer it into another device, such as your own computer or Blackberry) can violate local wiretapping laws. Other states make it illegal to intercept a computer communication "while it is in transit." Spyware may accomplish this type of interception without you realizing it.

Be Careful: Many divorce court judges won't accept "improperly" obtained information as evidence in a divorce action.

Internet and computer technology laws are constantly evolving. This issue poses a legal gray area for the courts, since judges are still hashing out what kind of conduct constitutes a crime. To avoid becoming one of their test cases, best to err on the side of caution when conducting your marital asset investigation via a computer search by consulting with an attorney.

Run Your Husband's Credit Report

Your husband's credit report is the ultimate paper trail. The report reveals marital debts, personal debts, lawsuits, and bankruptcy filings, as well as any bills he has neglected to pay. Educate yourself on what he owes so you don't get stuck paying his bills after the divorce, since ex-wives can sometimes be held responsible for their spouses' debt if it was accrued during the marriage.

Be Careful: You must have your husband's consent to run his report. Once you do, you can order a free credit report off the Internet from nationwide consumer reporting companies by providing your husband's social security number, address, and date of birth at www.AnnualCreditReport.com.

The Mail

To prepare for potential surprises in divorce court, many women start reading their husband's incoming mail. Credit card bills, bank account statements, purchase invoices, frequent flier mile statements, cashed check statements, and cell phone bills usually contain loads of relevant information. Many of these items can also be extremely helpful in uncovering whether he is having an affair.

Be Careful: By opening his mail you may be breaking the law, even if you are his wife. Opening letters or packages delivered by the U.S. Postal Service that are not addressed to you can constitute a criminal offense.

This may sound strange, but after your husband reads his mail, if he discards the contents of the envelopes in the trash, it's fair game. You can examine whatever he throws away. Private investigators search curbside garbage all the time looking for clues or evidence for various court cases.

Hire a Money Detective

If your asset search leads to a dead end, don't worry. There are professionals who can help you locate money and property. *Forensic accountants* serve as "financial detectives" and specialize in following paper trails and scrutinizing transaction records. Attorneys often hire them in divorce cases when one spouse has hidden money from the other or has engaged in complex financial maneuvers for his own benefit.

The expert services of forensic accountants aren't cheap. Their fees average between two hundred and four hundred dollars an hour. But if you believe there are significant marital assets, it is worth spending money to find them. Ask your accountant or attorney to refer you to a forensic specialist, seek referrals from divorced friends, or consult the Internet or Yellow Pages.

Some women learn from their asset searches that their household income is much higher than their husbands had led them to believe, and they feel cheated. I know a wife who treated herself to new jewelry and wardrobe in order to spend her husband's money in anticipation of filing for divorce. Once the papers were served and her husband realized what she had done, he raised the issue in front of the judge. The wife was forced to take a smaller property settlement after the costs of the items she purchased were deducted from her share of the marital assets.

 **Be Careful:** Don't start charging up a storm or going on wild spending sprees to make up for your "deprivation" during the marriage. Judges recognize when spouses unfairly help themselves to marital assets and punish accordingly.

Performing a successful marital property search really strengthens your position in a divorce action. Plus, don't forget that if you do the work yourself early on, it's less likely that you will have to pay a lawyer to locate what might have already been within reach.

CHAPTER 4
Eight Insider Tips on What to Do Once Your Divorce Begins

As soon as the divorce begins, shield your assets and possessions from your spouse, and revoke his legal authority to manage or control your affairs. It is crucial to prevent him from taking more than he is entitled to, running up household bills, making the wrong decisions on your behalf, or injuring your credit. If you don't act quickly, your spouse may attempt to deprive you of your fair share of property and assets in a divorce settlement. Sometimes the maneuvering isn't caught until it's too late, and valuables are already gone for good. Either cash was spent and is untraceable, money was funneled away to a third party or a secret account, or missing property was hidden so well it's unrecoverable. While you may not be wealthy enough to worry whether your husband squirreled away assets in secret Cayman Island trusts or Swiss bank accounts, a greedy husband can do significant damage to your bottom line. Follow these eight essential insider tips to protect yourself, your money, and your property.

1. Freeze All Joint Accounts

As soon as your divorce begins, freeze all joint bank accounts, brokerage accounts, trust accounts, and any other type of account to which your husband has access. This will prevent both parties from withdrawing any money or wasting marital assets until your financial affairs are settled in divorce court.

Send a certified letter to banks and other financial institutions authorizing them to freeze the accounts due to a pending divorce action. Some banks will not accept written requests and require you to get a court order authorizing a hold on funds.

Freezing an account does not affect the outcome of how the contents are distributed once a marriage is terminated. It simply preserves the marital assets while the divorce is pending. The funds in an account can eventually be "unfrozen" via an additional formal request when it's time to officially divide your property.

Strategy Tip: Let your husband know when you have frozen an account so he doesn't feel ambushed when he tries to access funds.

2. File Paperwork to Protect Assets, Property, and Legal Rights

Once a divorce begins, a wife can protect herself from her husband's potentially damaging strategies or maneuvers by filing paperwork with the court called a *motion*. A motion is a written request for court intervention or assistance that a judge will either *grant* or *deny*. Either spouse can file a motion, as long as a divorce action is open and pending.

Sometimes motions are filed as a type of pre-emptive strike before an opposing spouse has actually done anything improper, to prevent potentially harmful future conduct. For example, a motion can serve to protect property from disappearing after divorce papers are filed—a typical time when some husbands will start to improperly dispose of marital assets. For a pre-emptive motion to be granted, in most states you must show a judge that there is a danger of *irreparable harm,* requiring your husband's conduct to be "restrained" *before* he has an opportunity to act. This strategy tactic is utilized if you have evidence or information that your husband is planning on manipulating the family finances to increase his chances of getting a better divorce settlement.

In most states, there is little limitation on the type of issues you can ask the court to resolve, as long as your motion request is reasonable and not frivolous. Some common issues addressed via motions may involve seeking a court order preventing a spouse from selling a family heirloom, requiring him to purchase items for a special needs child, or forcing the return of furniture improperly removed from the marital home. Here is a closer look at the standard types of motions typically filed in divorce court:

- **Motion to Shield Marital Assets and Property**
  If you have located marital property during a Pre-Divorce Plan search, how do you protect your share once the divorce

is under way? By filing a *Motion to Shield Marital Assets,* sometimes called a *Temporary Restraining Order,* an *Order to Show Cause,* or a *Pendente Lite Motion.* A court can intercede upon request and freeze brokerage accounts or bank accounts in cases where a court order is required, or order your husband to refrain from selling the family home until the divorce is finalized. These motions are crucial to stopping a husband from taking more than he is entitled to.

Be Careful: While you are married, you and your spouse are generally free to sell your personal property and your marital property without the other's consent. But once divorce papers are served, spouses should avoid making unilateral financial decisions that affect joint marital assets. The untimely sale of marital possessions will be subject to court scrutiny. When a marriage is being dissolved, it is improper to dispose of assets without a spouse's consent or transfer property to family or friends where your spouse can't find it, even if you believe the property ultimately belongs to you. Both spouses must wait for their divorce case to be resolved before they will have a final, official decision on who keeps what property.

- **Motion for a Temporary Restraining Order on a Safe or Safe-Deposit Box**
  If you believe your husband is harboring marital property in his safe or safe-deposit box, you can ask the court to impound that safe and allow you access to inventory the contents. A safe is an especially good place to look for tangible valuables, like cash and

jewelry, documentation of assets, titles to property, and other important legal paperwork. This type of motion is particularly helpful when items appear to be missing after you complete the property inventory portion of your Pre-Divorce Plan.

• **Motion for Exclusive Use of the Family Car**
If your husband is interfering with your use of the family car, you can ask the court to award you *exclusive use* of the vehicle.

Here's a situation I witnessed during my practice where such a motion proved useful. A vindictive husband, angry over his imminent divorce, sent a tow truck to his wife's workplace. He had her car repossessed from the school parking lot directly outside her first-grade classroom. The teacher was forced to ride the train and a connecting bus line to get home that day.

She immediately filed a motion with the court explaining that personal transportation was a necessity for her livelihood and asked for judicial intervention. Even though the car was leased in her husband's name, the judge found she would suffer hardship without transportation to work and issued a *Temporary Order* forcing him to return it to her without delay.

Be Careful: If a court awards you property *temporarily* while your divorce is pending, the item in question may eventually have to be turned over to your ex as part of property distribution when the divorce is finalized. If your husband insists on keeping the property or is entitled to keep it after the divorce, make sure to negotiate a cash-equivalent or suitable replacement as part of your divorce settlement.

• **Motion for Temporary Payment of Medical Expenses**
If you or your child have special health needs and require
additional funds to pay for the cost of non-reimbursed medical
expenses, such as large co-payments, medical equipment, or
prescriptions, file a motion requesting that your spouse be
ordered to pay or at least contribute to the bills. These motions
are particularly successful if he is the primary breadwinner.

Although the ultimate responsibility for these types of
expenses should be re-addressed when you negotiate your divorce
agreement, securing a temporary court order in the meantime will
help relieve financial stress until the issue can be resolved.

3. Cancel Joint Credit Cards

Cancel any joint credit cards at the onset of your divorce. This
will prevent your husband from incurring new debt for which
you could be held responsible after the divorce. Because you
have obtained your own credit card as part of your Pre-Divorce
Plan, credit will still be available to you.

4. Stay in the Family Home if You Want to Keep It

The question I am asked most by wives on the verge of divorce or
already engaged in the process is: *"Is it okay for me to move out of our
house before we file divorce papers or once the divorce is under way?"*

Some lawyers will tell you it's okay to leave if that's what
will make your divorce easier emotionally. But I disagree. *If you
leave the house, you may lose it.*

Regardless of when the divorce papers are filed or who initiated the divorce, do *not* move out, "temporarily" stay with a friend or relative, or take a "cooling-off period" away from home.

In most states, while the divorce is pending, courts like to freeze the status quo. There's a higher likelihood that whoever is in the house at the time of the divorce will probably get to stay there, and even get to keep the house once the divorce is finalized. This is especially true for mothers who are the primary caretakers for children. Courts are reluctant to interrupt children's schooling and favor keeping them in a familiar environment.

If you leave, you may be viewed as "abandoning the home" and be forced to relinquish your right to the property. If you are a parent and leave the children to live in the home with their father, you may prejudice your case for child custody. The only reason to leave is if you feel physically threatened, or if you are in immediate danger from your spouse.

Bonus Tip: After filing for divorce, if you remain in the house without your husband, file a special motion with the court, asking that your husband be ordered to pay the mortgage until things are sorted out. Courts will usually grant this request when the husband is the sole breadwinner.

How to Keep Peace in the Valley

"What do I do if my spouse refuses to leave the home after we decide to divorce?"

If your husband refuses to vacate your home during a divorce (remember, if he were getting advice from a lawyer, he, too, would be told to stay put), you may need to adjust to living with him as your housemate under trying emotional circumstances. Sometimes a bit of creativity is needed to keep the peace.

I know one couple who hired a carpenter to erect a wall down the middle of their living room while they both, under advice of counsel, remained in the house during the divorce proceedings. Living separate lives under the same roof without having to see each other gave them the breathing room they needed to survive their one-year divorce action without killing each other. Couples who *choose* to stay in the house together during a divorce have other options, perhaps less extreme than home reconstruction. If the extra space is available, each can take their own bedroom and make an effort to stay out of the other's way.

****

Take It from Someone Who Knows: In my own divorce, my husband not only stayed in the house, but he also refused to vacate the master bedroom suite, which had a Jacuzzi bathtub, walk-in closet, dressing area, built-in makeup vanity, and fireplace. To avoid him, I had no choice but to move into a tiny guest bedroom until the divorce was settled.

I took the high road and the small room. It was more important to me to save my energy for property division negotiations than to fight over my temporary living quarters. So what if my husband got the better room for a few months; I got the better deal in the divorce.

****

If you have a one-bedroom home or apartment, and he refuses to give up the bedroom or move out, I suggest buying yourself a quality air mattress and converting the living room into your bedroom. Advise your spouse that the living room is now yours, and is off-limits. Move your clothing into the hallway closet and, if need be, buy a cheap throwaway bureau to store your stuff. Even extra kitchen cabinets can serve as a useful place to put your belongings in a pinch.

Be Careful: If you and your husband both remain in the home, and he subsequently places you in physical danger, is physically or emotionally abusive, or threatens you, there is a remedy. You can file for an emergency *restraining order* or an *order of protection* (also called a *protective order*, depending on your state), which will effectively remove him from the house. These types of orders forbid a spouse from coming into physical contact with you or force him to stay a certain distance away. With a restraining order, he will have no choice but to vacate.

If your husband continues to make contact with you despite a court order, he can be arrested and charged with a criminal offense, either a misdemeanor or felony, depending on your state laws. If convicted, he may be punished with probation, an anger management program, or even jail time.

5. Make a Record

If your husband engages in inappropriate behavior during your divorce that can affect the financial outcome of your case or the well-being of your children, keep a journal, diary, or written log of his questionable conduct. Record dates, times, and descriptions of his activities. Excessive drinking or drug use, criminal activity, mistreatment or neglect of the children, or suspicious business transactions may prove to be valuable evidence in divorce court.

Written notes particularly come in handy in child custody battles. If your husband fails to show up to pick up the kids, returns them late from visitation, or acts inappropriately in front of them, you can cite his conduct as a reason for requesting a modification of custody or visitation orders. The more details you have, the more convincing your case will be.

Even if you are not sure of the significance of his conduct now, if it raises a red flag for you, it may be relevant down the road in divorce court, so write it down!

6. Remove Your Personal Property from the House

Protect your valuable personal property from disappearing during a divorce by removing it from the home for safekeeping. Jewelry, items with sentimental value, or your family heirlooms may be pocketed by a vindictive husband. To avoid this, move property to a personal safe-deposit box or put it in the trust of a family member.

7. Revoke Any Powers of Attorney Given to Your Spouse

A power of attorney is a legal document authorizing a party to conduct legal transactions on behalf of another. If you have granted your husband a power of attorney in the past (attorneys often prepare and present these documents for couples to sign along with the drafting of their wills), he may still have authority to sell your real estate, secure loans in your name, or withdraw money from your bank account. See an attorney immediately to prepare a new document revoking your spouse's power of attorney and send a copy to your spouse.

8. Revise Your Health Care Instructions

Many wives no longer want their husbands in charge of their affairs once a divorce is under way, especially when it comes to making crucial health care decisions. If that is also your sentiment, remove your husband's name from any legal document putting authority for your health care or medical treatment in his hands. Revoke and revise your *health care affidavit* or *health care proxy* to authorize a different individual to issue medical directives on your behalf in the event you suffer a devastating illness that renders you incapable.

By now you have set yourself up in a position of strength before the divorce by implementing the Pre-Divorce Plan, and by following these important steps during the divorce, you are further boosting your chances for divorce success. Taking proactive steps to shift the balance of power back to you, and preparing for any future obstacles that might come your way, should go a long way to help you feel a bit less anxious and a lot more confident as the process proceeds.

CHAPTER 5
Whose Fault Is It, Anyway?
Fault Divorce, No-Fault Divorce, and Legal Separation

There are two types of divorces, *fault* and *no-fault*. In a *fault* divorce, a spouse seeking divorce must prove *grounds*, or legal reasons, why the other spouse is at fault for causing the marriage to fail. The defending spouse can stop a fault divorce from happening by disagreeing with the grounds and convincing the court that he or she is not at fault. In a *no-fault* divorce, no legal accusation of blame is placed. Spouses who file for a no-fault divorce will always get one, regardless of who is at fault.

Whether you are eligible to file for a fault or a no-fault divorce depends on the laws of the state where your divorce is filed. As of the writing of this book, at least fifteen states have laws that permit only no-fault divorces, including Arizona, California, Colorado, Florida, Indiana, Iowa, Kansas, Kentucky, Michigan, Missouri, Montana, Nebraska, Washington, Wisconsin, and Wyoming. Other states recognize fault divorce laws, but will allow a no-fault divorce after a couple separates for a specified period of time (in some states the period is as long as two years).

Couples who don't want to wait the required separation period often opt for a fault divorce with the hope of getting divorced quicker. New York, known as the strictest divorce state in the country, is the only state that doesn't recognize a true no-fault divorce law.

Grounds for Divorce

In a no-fault divorce, a couple merely alleges grounds of *irretrievable breakdown, incompatibility,* or *irreconcilable differences* in their divorce papers, depending on what language their state's law requires. Since neither spouse is considered legally at fault for the breakup, no one has to prove the grounds in court.

But the same does not hold true in a fault divorce. One party must be singled out for blame in the divorce papers, even if the allegations of fault are unflattering or embarrassing. If a relationship ended by mutual consent and no one was really at fault, couples sometimes feel forced to select a fictitious legal reason why the marriage failed, just to get their case moving through the court system.

Here's a sampling of grounds that can be alleged against a spouse who is "at fault."

Misrepresentation

There was a *misrepresentation* made by one spouse, which induced the other to enter the marriage. For example, a spouse who stated he or she wanted children before marriage and then refuses to have children made a misrepresentation that provides the other spouse with a legal ground for divorce.

Incurable insanity
One of the parties has an incurable mental illness interfering with their participation in the marriage.

Failure to consummate the marriage
The parties never had sex from the day they were married.

Adultery
Allegations of cheating can be raised in the courtroom.

Abandonment
This occurs when one spouse walks out, without justification or the other's consent, and doesn't return. Abandonment is also implied when a spouse, through his conduct, indicates that there is no intention to resume the marital relationship. Each state has its own requirement of how long the period of abandonment must be before the divorce action can be initiated.

When a spouse permanently stops having sexual relations with his or her partner, this is sometimes called "constructive abandonment," and it constitutes a ground for divorce.

Cruel and inhuman treatment
This involves either physical or mental cruelty. To be a ground for divorce, the cruelty must be so significant that it is unsafe or inappropriate for the parties to continue the marriage. Some examples of cruel or inhuman treatment are physical attacks,

verbal abuse, dating another man or woman, or gambling away marital assets or household funds. Some courts hold that the longer the marriage, the more egregious the mistreatment must be for a spouse to substantiate this ground.

Alcoholism or mental illness alone is usually not considered cruel and inhuman treatment. But if a spouse becomes violent when intoxicated or mistreats the other due to mental health issues, his or her actions may serve as a ground for divorce.

Nonsupport

A spouse refuses to financially support the other or the household.

Jail or prison time

If a spouse is sentenced to a lengthy prison term and is no longer "available" to participate in the legal union, the incarceration serves as a legal reason for ending the marriage. Each individual state's laws specify how long the jail term must be to constitute a ground for divorce.

Extra Attention Required: Check with an attorney if you need help determining which ground might apply in your case. If you are handling your own divorce, some states have free forms in the local divorce court clerk's office that can assist you in assessing the appropriate ground.

How Do You Prove Grounds?

To prove grounds, most courts accept sworn testimony by the plaintiff (the spouse who filed the divorce) verifying the reason for the breakup. If the defending spouse challenges the stated ground as being untrue, a court battle will ensue. In those cases, both spouses will usually give testimony and/or present evidence to support their respective positions.

How Long Is My Divorce Going to Take?

The pace at which a fault or a no-fault divorce proceeds depends on whether the divorce action is *contested* (challenged) or *uncontested* (unchallenged). A contested divorce occurs when:

1. there's no agreement on one or more of the dissolution "issues" (spousal support, child support, child custody, visitation, and property division)
2. one spouse does not agree to getting divorced
3. the defendant is challenging the grounds alleged for the divorce (in a fault state)

Even if a couple resolves one or more of their disputed issues during the divorce action, if disagreement remains on any other, the divorce will still be considered contested. Depending on the state where it's filed and the level of conflict between the spouses, a contested divorce can take up to a year or more to complete.

In an *uncontested divorce*, both spouses agree to get divorced, and there are no disputes as to dissolution "issues." Uncontested actions proceed more quickly, because there's less litigation involved and few, if any, court appearances required. These divorce actions are often accomplished with the filing of paperwork. In some cases, they are simple enough that a lawyer isn't necessary.

What Is a Legal Separation, and How Will It Affect My Divorce?

In some states, before a divorce can go forward, a *separation* is required. When that is the case, a couple must physically separate for a specified period of time. Other states with this requirement demand a formal legal separation, which is achieved by filing a written *separation contract, separation agreement,* or *judgment of separation* with the court. During separation, the parties agree to live separately while still legally married, and to determine issues of temporary child custody, visitation and support, temporary spousal maintenance, and sometimes property division. Once the required separation period passes, couples are then permitted to file a divorce petition. Some fault states will make an exception and allow a divorce to go forward without proof of grounds if the couple files a legal separation agreement and lives apart for a specified period of time.

Other states have no separation requirement, but instead demand that couples take a "cooling-off period" before a divorce will be granted. For example, in Connecticut, the law requires a three-month wait after divorce papers are filed before couples are permitted to divorce. The reason the courts delay the process is to see if the spouses will change their minds before making the breakup permanent.

Extra Attention Required: Contact a divorce attorney or your local court clerk's office for your state's requirements.

Couples who are not yet sure a divorce is the right path for them will sometimes informally separate without court intervention. The marriage remains legally intact, and the self-imposed period of separation will have no impact on how quickly a divorce action can proceed if it is eventually filed. This type of separation merely allows spouses to take a breather from the marriage and to assess whether divorce is the correct option.

As you can see, couples don't always get to choose the method and manner by which they enter the divorce process. State law controls when a divorce can be filed, the pace of the process, and how hard it is to actually get divorced. No matter where you get divorced or what type of divorce you file, keep in mind that the legal system has not been designed to comfort or cushion the range of human emotion that accompanies a divorce lawsuit. The next chapter will help you prepare emotionally for the divorce battle.

CHAPTER 6
How to Shape Up for the Divorce Battle

Being a party to a lawsuit is an emotionally draining experience. I have heard people compare the feeling of going through a divorce to getting the wind knocked out of you. Many spouses suffer from anxiety or depression while their divorce is under way.

While a marriage is under siege, we need to focus on maintaining our physical and mental health and preserving our stamina to make it through the process. Gather your strength to fight for what you deserve, because it may be your last chance to get the financial support you need to make it on your own.

The Divorce Diet

How many women do you know who have been on the "Divorce Diet?" They get so consumed with the divorce or frazzled from the intensity of the legal action that they forget to eat. I have witnessed friends shed pounds like water because of stress from their legal battles. Many were thrilled with the results of their unintended weight loss, but rapid shrinkage caused by nerves is not the way to go. Pay attention to your personal maintenance, eating habits, and nutrition in order to maintain your health and stamina throughout the legal battle.

Let's Get Physical

Sweating out your anxiety is a great way to shape up for the divorce. Physical activity burns off steam and has been proven to reduce stress. Exercise, yoga, and meditation are known to alleviate anxiety and help you sleep better. If the company your husband works for offers corporate or group discounts on gym memberships, take advantage of that until the divorce is finalized, since you are still legally married and should have access to his benefits.

Bonus Tip: If membership fees for group athletics or health clubs seem too expensive, it may be possible to eventually "bill" your husband for the expense. When it comes time to divide money, assets, and property, you can negotiate with him to pay your monthly health club bills as part of your settlement agreement. Some wives have even successfully convinced their soon-to-be ex-husbands to cover the costs of therapy, acupuncture, spa treatments, and tennis lessons.

Join a Group

If you are feeling depressed, take action. The better you feel, the better you will handle your divorce litigation. Try to surround yourself with people who can fill the void or calm the restlessness that often takes over during a separation. Overcome loneliness by joining a book club, a museum group, a library group, or a class.

Find a Therapist

When a husband moves out, loneliness, fear of isolation, or feelings of abandonment can trigger panic attacks or anxiety. If you become overwhelmed, counseling or therapy may be necessary to get you through the divorce process.

The question that usually arises is, "How do I pay for this service during a divorce, when money is tighter than usual?" Some therapists offer a sliding fee scale depending on your income, so don't be afraid to ask if they will charge you less than their normal hourly rate.

Bonus Tip: Therapy bills are another expense you may want to negotiate with your husband to pay. It may be easier to convince him to foot the bills if *he* dumped *you*. If you're not shy about letting him know you are having a hard time coping with his decision, you may be able to "guilt" him into writing the check.

Find a Divorce Support Group

If you cannot afford therapy, spend some time researching community centers, or go online to find a divorce support group in your area. Some are free and others charge a nominal fee to join.

You can seek support online from other women engaged in the battle at www.HeHadItComingBook.com, which hosts a virtual divorce support community.

Lean on Your Divorced Friends

Seek the support of a friend who has gone through the divorce process or is going through it at the same time as you. It's so much easier to cope and certainly more comforting when we have a sympathetic ear, particularly in the form of a friend who has "been there, done that." A divorcée possesses a unique insight on life, relationships, and marriage as a result of navigating the divorce process. With a 50 percent divorce rate, it shouldn't be hard to find a pal in a similar predicament.

CHAPTER 7
From Wedding Ring to Boxing Ring: What to Expect in a Divorce Lawsuit

A divorce is merely a lawsuit that dissolves the legal contract existing between spouses. The process is actually manageable once you learn the mechanics of a divorce lawsuit and how a case proceeds through the legal system. A legal action becomes more complicated (and costly) when couples refuse to compromise and drag their case through the system for many months and even years. Once you know the mechanics of how divorce works and what to expect, you can take charge of your case, reduce conflict with your spouse, implement your strategy, cut your costs, and win!

Who's Who in a Divorce Lawsuit

If you initiate the lawsuit, you are the *plaintiff* (or *petitioner*). If you are served with divorce papers, you automatically become the *defendant* (or *respondent*) to the action. Some attorneys believe plaintiffs have a tactical advantage because they present their case first. Others believe it doesn't matter who gets sued and who does the suing, because each party will be given an equal opportunity to present their case in court.

In my opinion, if you have the opportunity to file first, take it. I prefer to lead the direction of the case by presenting my client's version of the facts first. However, if your husband files first, you are not at any disadvantage. In fact, the benefit is that he, as the plaintiff, will be solely responsible for paying the filing and service fees.

All He Ever Did Was "Complain(t)"

The *divorce complaint* (sometimes called an *information* or a *petition*) is the document that initiates a divorce lawsuit. A complaint presents information about your marriage in the form of unproven statements known as *allegations*.

Typical Allegations Contained in a Divorce Complaint

- a statement that the parties are legally married
- a statement indicating when and where the marriage occurred
- a confirmation that both spouses are *legal residents* of the state, as well as the specific county, borough, or township where the action is filed, giving the court *jurisdiction* to dissolve the marriage
- *grounds* or legal reasons why a judge should grant your divorce, such as "The marriage is irretrievably broken" or "The defendant committed adultery"
- a statement of the number of children produced by the marriage
- a formal request for the court to dissolve the marriage

You must file your divorce complaint in the state where you are considered a *legal resident*, not in the state where you were married (unless, of course, they are the same). To be a legal resident, you must meet a state's residency requirement by permanently residing there for a specified period of time. (California calls it a *domicile* requirement.) Anywhere from six months to one year is typical, but a few states allow as little as three months. Alaska, South Dakota, and Washington are the only states that have no required time period. You just have to be a resident of the state at the time you file.

 Extra Attention Required: If you recently relocated, check with your courthouse clerk to make sure you are eligible to file in that jurisdiction.

 Strategy Tip: If your spouse has moved out of state, file for divorce first to ensure that the legal action proceeds in your home state rather than his newly established state of residence.

Making It Legal

The paperwork needed to start a divorce, what most people call the "divorce papers," consists of the *complaint* and a *summons*, or in some states just a summons alone. A summons is a legal document "summoning" the defendant to make a personal appearance in divorce court to respond to the allegations in the complaint or instructing him or her to file a written response, called an *answer*, by a certain date in lieu of a court appearance.

A summons is *served* when it is formally handed to a spouse by a person who is recognized by the jurisdiction as having legal authority to serve lawsuits. Some states allow your divorce lawyer to serve papers on your spouse's divorce lawyer, or permit service by mail. Others require that it be done by a licensed process server, who physically hands the defendant the papers. If you are handling your divorce on your own, you can talk to the divorce court clerk to learn how proper legal service is achieved in your state.

Don't Ambush Your Spouse

Be considerate, as well as strategic, when arranging for *service of process*. How you initiate your divorce often sets the tone for the subsequent proceedings. Service made in a public place (such as at your spouse's office) can be dramatic and embarrassing. He may retaliate during the divorce action if he feels that you humiliated him. I recommend having him served in private, where the server goes to his home, knocks on the door, and hands him the papers.

****

Take It from Someone Who Knows: I let my husband know exactly how the procedure would work the day before service was to occur. I didn't want to "ambush" him and start my divorce off with bad blood. (I had already told him I would be filing for divorce a few days earlier.) I informed him that between eight and nine the next morning, a sheriff would knock at our front door. He was to open the door and take the papers the sheriff was holding. In the papers he would be named as a defendant, and there would be instructions on what he should do next.

When he was served, my husband was a bit shaken, but he handled it well. My explanation of the process before it occurred showed him respect and proved to be effective in calming his nerves, helping him to trust me, and allowing for an amicable divorce action.

****

Service Evaders

It's not always an easy task to get your divorce papers served. Some husbands have attempted to avoid service of process at all costs to make their wives' lives as difficult as possible. One soon-to-be ex-husband would exit his house through the back door and cross through a neighbor's backyard to evade the server. He would come and go at odd and unpredictable times to prolong the process. Finally, when the process server had no choice but to go to his workplace, the husband refused to come to the reception area to receive the papers, shielding himself through his secretary.

Finally the server got creative. One day the husband left the house and tried to drive away in his car, with his windows open. The server rolled the divorce papers up like a newspaper, secured them with a rubber band, and flung the packet through the open passenger window. The "fling" constituted legal service of process, and the defendant had been served.

Answer Me!

Every defendant is required to *answer* a divorce lawsuit once he or she is served. The answer is a line-by-line response to the allegations in the complaint, stating whether you agree or disagree with what's stated. Typical answers are "I admit," "I deny," or "I don't have enough information to respond." If both parties agree that an allegation in the complaint is true, there will be no litigation on that point, and the court will accept it as a fact. If parties disagree on divorce allegations, they may litigate the disputed facts.

Once an answer is filed, your divorce action will be under way and headed on a path toward final dissolution. You will either resolve your case outside of court and send written agreements and paperwork to the judge for approval, or your divorce issues will require a more time-consuming remedy—a trip to divorce court.

CHAPTER 8

How to Navigate Divorce Court: Taking Your Case Through Hearings and Trial

When a couple can't agree on how their property will be divided, who will pay spousal support and how much, or issues regarding the children, the filing and serving of paperwork will not be enough to get them divorced. The case will move to the courthouse, where spouses will be required to litigate their unresolved issues in front of a judge.

An issue or disagreement is brought to a judge's attention when you or your lawyer files legal paperwork known as a *motion* (also called an *application, order to show cause,* or *request for a court order*, depending on your state). (Several examples of motion filing were discussed in Chapter 4.) Motions provide an opportunity for court intervention on issues that need immediate resolution while the divorce is pending. For example, if a husband stops paying child support or mortgage payments on the family home, or refuses to support a stay-at-home mom while the divorce is pending, the wife can file a motion to request a court hearing to fix the problem. The more motions filed in a case, the more litigation required, and the more expensive your divorce will be if you have a divorce attorney.

What Am I Hearing?

Once a motion is filed, both spouses are required to appear in court to attend a legal *hearing* on the issues raised in the motion papers. Hearings are like mini-trials that occur before a divorce trial and deal with individual issues instead of the whole case. In the courtroom, the party who filed the motion will present arguments or evidence supporting the motion to the judge. The opposing party is allowed to defend the motion by rebutting the evidence or arguing against the reasons presented by their spouse as to why the motion should be granted. The judge listens to both sides and makes a decision, called a *ruling* or an *order*, letting the parties know with whom he or she agrees and/or what they are required to do.

Sometimes, with simple matters, a hearing won't be necessary. A judge will read your motion on his or her own and then read your husband's *response* or *objection*, and make an immediate decision. But the majority of motions are argued "live" in front of a judge, with both parties' attendance required. On motion hearing days, be prepared to possibly spend an entire day in court waiting for your case to be heard. If a spouse does not show up to a motion hearing day, he or she will lose the issue by default, even if they had a strong case.

When Trial Is Necessary

If a couple's disputes requiring immediate attention are resolved through motion hearings, but they still can't agree on remaining divorce issues, such as permanent spousal support (alimony or maintenance), custody, and property division, the case will go to *trial*, the final stage of the litigation process. At a divorce trial, just like any other trial, evidence is presented to the court, witnesses are called to the stand, and arguments are made to convince the judge whether to accept the plaintiff's or the defendant's side of the story. (There are no juries in divorce cases.) Once the spouses present all their evidence and testimony, and "rest their cases," a judge will decide all outstanding divorce issues.

Be Careful: If you haven't hired an attorney and your divorce reaches the trial stage, it's time to seek legal assistance to handle the courtroom proceedings.

What Does It Take to "Prove" a Divorce Case?

If your divorce goes before a judge for trial, you must prove your side of the case with evidence. Evidence can be used to prove the value of marital assets, what your lifestyle or standard of living is like, who would make a better custodial parent to the children, why one spouse should keep the house, or why a wife deserves alimony. There are two types of evidence: *testimonial evidence* (testimony derived from what people say) and *physical evidence* (which is tangible and can be touched or viewed).

Testimonial evidence is admitted into a court record when a witness or party to a legal action gets on the stand and testifies under oath. If a witness is *credible*, the legal term for "believable," the judge will accept the testimony as true and make legal decisions based on it. Physical evidence is displayed to the judge and introduced into the record, becoming part of your court case file.

Examples of testimonial evidence

- sworn, oral statements made by a spouse
- sworn, oral statements made by a witness
- sworn, oral statements made by an expert
- written or recorded statements made under special circumstances by a witness who is not available to come to court

Examples of physical evidence

- video
- documents
- reports
- photographs
- bills and receipts
- pay stubs
- bank account statements

For contentious or complex divorce cases, the introduction of outside witnesses (third-party witnesses) may be necessary to provide extra proof. Several types of witnesses can sway a judge's opinion in your favor at a divorce trial:

- Your accountant, to testify about financial issues
- Your babysitter, to discuss the needs of the children or your husband's compliance with the visitation schedule
- An appraiser, to state the value of your house or to disprove the validity of your husband's own appraiser's report
- Your neighbor, who witnessed your husband's inappropriate behavior, conduct, or activities at the marital home
- A bank teller, to testify that your husband misappropriated funds from the joint account
- Your family members, to corroborate that your husband was verbally or physically abusive to you or the children

Extra Attention Required: The downside of using an expert witness or professional witness (accountants, doctors, psychologists, appraisers, etc.) is the expense, since they must be "hired" for their court appearances. They charge by the hour and will bill you not only for the time needed to give their testimony, but for the time they may have to wait in the courthouse until it is their turn to take the stand, as well as their travel time to and from court. You may want to consult with your attorney about the expected effectiveness of a hired witness before you agree to spend the money. However, if you are unemployed and your husband is the only wage earner, your lawyer can ask the court to order your spouse to pay the fees.

The Final Answer

After evidence is presented to the judge, he or she will then weigh and balance both sets of testimonial and/or physical evidence to determine which is more truthful, accurate, or reliable, and which will be accepted as fact. A judge makes a decision on how to resolve the contested marital issues based on his or her interpretation of the evidence and issues a final order outlining the decisions that the parties must follow. The couple will now be on their way to getting divorced.

The Final Appearance

Even if your divorce action was amicable and uncontested, you are not entirely exempt from appearing in divorce court. In most states, whether or not your case went to trial, you and your spouse are required to make a court appearance at the end of all the proceedings, called a *dissolution hearing, termination hearing,* or *final hearing.* This is where the judge will approve the final drafted divorce agreement. If there are no outstanding issues between you, the hearing is a quick, perfunctory matter. After the court reviews that all the papers are in order and signed by you and your spouse, the judge will grant the divorce.

But there's still one more hurdle. You are not legally divorced until the judge signs and stamps your dissolution agreement. In some states you will have to wait for the court clerk to mail you the finalized divorce papers with the judge's signature. In other states you are divorced as soon as the hearing ends, if the judge signs off on the spot.

An Insider's Guide to Making a Successful Court Appearance

Mind Your Manners

It's important to obtain and maintain the judge's respect. You should be on your best behavior whenever you are in a divorce courtroom. Your conduct and presentation will be scrutinized by the judge and factored into the final result. If you act out, throw tantrums, scream, or interrupt, you will quickly get on the judge's bad side and risk hurting your case. In reality, when both sides present equally strong cases, where the gavel will fall sometimes depends on who made the better impression. (For more on how to control your emotions in court, see Chapter 9.)

You should also be prepared that if your case ends up tried in a jurisdiction with an "open courtroom" policy, anything you say and do in court is also on display for the community. Bad behavior will be witnessed and dirty laundry will be aired in front of whoever is in the audience.

Dress to Impress

What you wear to court counts. Dress as if you are going to a house of worship. Be well groomed. A blazer, conservative sweater, or dress is best.

That being said, if your lifestyle is expensive, dress the part. Show the judge what you are accustomed to. When he or she determines the amount of your alimony or property award, you want that decision to be expensive too . . . for your husband!

Be on Time

The judge expects you to be inside the courtroom at your scheduled time. On court days, reschedule any work or personal obligations that could interfere with your prompt arrival. If you are not in court when you should be, the judge could dismiss your motions and require you to refile, or make an unfavorable ruling without giving you a chance to respond.

Be Aware of the Nature of the Proceedings: Divorces Are Not Private

While information concerning minors is usually sealed, be aware that divorce actions in many states are considered matters of public record. In those jurisdictions that have an "open file" policy, once you file a complaint at the courthouse, anyone can take a peek at your file, including the media.

Bonus Tip: To protect your privacy on sensitive matters, some states allow you to request a "sealing order." If a "sealing order" is granted, the courtroom doors will literally be locked to the general public, and only the parties, their witnesses, and lawyers will be allowed inside.

Now that you know the nuts and bolts of navigating the legal system and what to expect behind courtroom doors, you should now feel the divorce court "intimidation factor" beginning to fade. The more you familiarize yourself with the mechanics of a divorce lawsuit, the better you can prepare your case.

CHAPTER 9
Don't Cry Out Loud:
How to Prevent Emotions from Weakening
Your Bargaining Power

Divorce brings out the worst in everyone, often turning husbands and wives into bitter enemies. It is crucial to maintain your composure both inside and outside of the courtroom. Otherwise, runaway emotions can rule the outcome of your future and ruin your divorce case. You don't want to blow it by blowing up.

I can't tell you it's easy to suppress the range of feelings that accompany divorce: loss, anger, insecurity, bitterness, hostility, regret, and rejection. But it's crucial to stay level and focused to be at the top of your game. Always keep your emotions in check. The best way to do this is to operate as if you are closing a business deal.

When divorcing spouses let anger or anxiety dictate their choices, they get overwhelmed and make bad decisions in the heat of the moment. Many women cave under the emotional strain of a divorce and throw in the towel too early, giving up important rights. Others explode in court, turning the judge against them. As a divorce attorney, I have witnessed parties lose control by screaming, cursing, wailing, and even leaping over the table to lunge at their spouse.

****

Take It From Someone Who Knows: During my divorce, keeping my cool and focusing my energy on the end result—rather than getting angry or confrontational—really paid off in the long run. Before my divorce was finalized, we had sold our home, and I returned for the final time to remove my possessions as well as my share of our furniture. I went over to the couch and began to fold up a blanket that we had kept draped over the back. The blanket was more of a couch throw that my mother had once given us as a house gift. It was special to me because she selected it, and the design reflected her unique taste and style. All in all, it was just a blanket, but to me it had sentimental value.

My soon-to-be-ex came over to me, grabbed the blanket out of my hands, and snarled, "I'm keeping it." I replied, "This was a gift from my family, so wouldn't it make sense that I would take it with me, since my mother picked it out?" He began yelling and refused to hand over the blanket. At that point I realized that my mental health, serenity, and stamina during the divorce were more important than any couch throw, so I left our home for the last time without my coveted blanket and didn't bring it up it again.

When the divorce was finalized, I had decided to forgive his maneuver with the blanket but still regretted not having it among my possessions. Two years later he called to tell me that he was remarrying, and I congratulated him. Then his voice became very soft and sweet. It was an "I need something from you" voice that I recognized from our married days. He said, "Stacy, in order to go ahead with my new marriage, I need for you to agree to participate in a get."

A *get* is a Jewish divorce that is conducted by a rabbi. Even if a judge has approved your divorce in a civil court of law, in the Jewish religion you are not considered a legitimately divorced couple without a get. Remarriage is forbidden for either spouse until a rabbi performs the sacred rituals and the couple executes the religious document of divorce known as the get.

As far as I was concerned, a judge in the state of Connecticut had legally divorced me. I had no urgency to obtain a get. But for my ex, it was another story. His rabbi would refuse to perform his marriage ceremony to his second bride unless he produced a get document signed by me. So I asked him, "May I have my blanket back now?" And he said, "No." So I responded, "No blanket, no get," and immediately hung up the phone. The next day, Federal Express delivered my blanket. It was well worth the wait, and I felt enormous pleasure from my belated victory.

****

How to Keep Your Emotions in Check

Count to Ten

You may remember this anxiety-soothing technique from childhood. When you feel yourself getting upset or anxious, or like you are about to unravel, stop what you are doing and silently count to ten. It's the equivalent of taking a personal time-out and works great to relieve tension while in the midst of conflict or heated argument. A ten-second break also gives you time to calm down and regroup.

A friend's husband was constantly insulting her and verbally provoking her throughout their settlement negotiation. Each time he offended her, she took a deep breath, silently counted to ten, and continued speaking as if nothing had happened. When the husband realized he wasn't going to get a reaction from her, he stopped. She was able to maintain her composure and continue working with him until they successfully hammered out an agreement.

Achieve Writer's Release

Another coping method that has worked well for divorcing women is to keep a journal. Expressing thoughts on paper is a positive and productive way to vent emotions and relieve frustration. It's also better to express rage in a notebook rather than directly to your spouse, who may retaliate by shutting down communications during the divorce. Writing is great therapy—and it's free.

Many women going through a divorce say mornings are the toughest time of the day. Their emotions come crashing down because they haven't yet faced the distractions of the day. Writing in a journal at the start of the day is a great way to release stress.

Be Careful: Don't advertise to your husband that you are keeping a journal. If your divorce gets really nasty, it's possible in some states for him or his lawyer to subpoena your journal. He may successfully convince a judge that it contains information relevant to a divorce issue, even if you started writing it after the divorce was filed. It's better that your husband doesn't know about your writing, so he doesn't think of going on an expedition to find it.

Practice deep breathing

Doctors tell their patients to take deep breaths during an anxiety attack. This also works well for divorce jitters. When your emotions start to overwhelm you, practice deep breathing to soothe your body and your mind.

Take a cooling-off period

Before making any drastic decisions or taking any risky action, stop and wait twenty-four hours. Take a reasonable cooling-off period. One night's sleep may completely change your perspective. You may wake up and realize that your potential conduct would only have embarrassed you or damaged whatever amicable relations are left between you and your spouse.

Pause before you act

I admit it. During a divorce, it feels good to vent. Many of us fantasize about *Desperate Housewives*-style behavior as a way to blow off steam during an emotionally charged divorce or as revenge against a mean-spirited spouse. Keep those fantasies in your head. If you lash out against him in real life, it's going to bring you real trouble in your divorce. Pause before you act to keep your emotions from influencing uncontrollable behavior.

Let's say a nagging feeling starts creeping up on you. You can barely contain yourself from phoning or e-mailing your husband and calling him every name in the book. Or you want to throw a rock through his window, key his car, or shred his business files. Think about what your words or actions will accomplish and how your spouse will respond. When you stop to recognize that your potential conduct is not going to produce a positive, desirable, or practical result and will only bring you hardship, you will think twice before picking up that phone or driving to his house.

In his anger during their divorce, actor Charlie Sheen apparently left vicious expletive-laced voice messages on his wife Denise Richards's answering machine. She produced a recording of his messages as evidence in court. Denise also claimed he made threats of violence against her, which he denied. The judge subsequently punished Sheen by ordering monitored visits with his children, and temporarily prevented the actor from coming within three hundred feet of his wife.

The Power of the Pause: Most parties to a divorce are already in a fragile emotional state. A simple pause in action can save you from additional heartache and headache. If at any time you crave contact or seek conflict with your spouse, think about what your potential words or actions will accomplish or how he might respond. Every action results in a reaction, and you may get a response that you don't want to hear during this emotionally trying time.

For example, let's say you are burning with anger and jealousy because your husband committed adultery, and you want to confront him about it. Stop, sit back, and have an internal dialogue with yourself. It might sound like this: "If I ring his doorbell and demand to know why he cheated on me during our marriage, what reaction or result will I get?"

You may be hoping for a response like this one:

"I made the most horrible mistake and I will never do it again. I want you back and I want us to drop all divorce proceedings. I will spend the rest of my life catering to your every wish and attempting to make this up to you."

But if you realistically answer your own question before you ask it out loud, you would more likely get a "reaction" similar to these:

1. He answers your question with a devastating effect: "I cheated on you because I stopped loving you ten years ago, and because you are unattractive and unappealing."
2. He calls the police and files a criminal trespass complaint against you to have you removed from his doorstep, or he files for a restraining order preventing you from visiting his home again if you get in his face.
3. He tells you to go to hell and slams the door in your face.
4. His girlfriend answers the door.

Before you reach out to him, determine what it is you are actually seeking. Is your potential contact really an excuse to get his attention? Are you really trying to ease your pain? Or, are you just lashing out? When considering taking a step that cannot result in a productive conclusion for your divorce action, there's reason to pause. Your intellect will kick in and warn you not to proceed. When you overrule your emotions with logic, you can avoid a potentially explosive emotional situation that will only impede your progress through this process. Why risk no gain, and only more pain?

No. You. Didn't.

Extreme behavior and acting out against a spouse can place you in jeopardy of becoming the subject of a restraining order or protective order (also called an order of protection in some states). These are court orders that "restrain" you from contact with your spouse. In many states, it is a crime to violate them. If you contact your spouse when it's forbidden, you could be hauled into court in handcuffs to face the judge. Your offensive conduct can have serious repercussions, including jail time.

If you unreasonably annoy, harass, or disturb your spouse with excessive phone calling, e-mailing, verbal or physical abuse, or by persistently showing up at his home or place of business uninvited, you may find yourself arrested for separate criminal charges, such as *harassment* or *stalking*. If you destroy or damage his property, you could be charged with a felony or misdemeanor for *criminal property damage, tampering,* or *criminal mischief* (depending on your state law).

It is humiliating and potentially damaging to your reputation to land in criminal court as a result of bad behavior during a divorce. Your name and fingerprints will be on file with the police station, and word of your alleged conduct could hit the local newspapers. Your permanent record could be stained if the court finds you have violated its order or convicts you of a crime. You may also be forced to attend court-mandated anger management programs or probation as punishment.

Either consequence would be a large burden for any woman holding down a job or raising kids on her own. (Obviously the same consequences hold true for your husband if he is the one doing the harassing.) The risk of incurring serious life-altering penalties is never worth the brief release gained from taking out your frustrations on your spouse. Throughout the divorce process, controlling your emotions and thinking before acting is always the best course of action.

CHAPTER 10

Getting "Affair" Settlement:
Capitalizing on Your Husband's Infidelity

Infidelity forces many women out of their marriages when they still love their spouses. If your husband appears to exit the relationship too comfortably or too easily, handles the prospect of divorce on a suspiciously steady emotional keel, or leaves you for no apparent reason, it's possible there is a third party in the picture. My mother's insight into extramarital affairs is compelling: *Men just don't pick up and leave the comfort of home for nothing. If they are suddenly gone, and you had no sign it was coming, you can bet he already has another woman in place.*

If you discover a girlfriend in the picture, be prepared for the divorce to take longer. Adultery creates additional financial and legal issues that can influence property division, support, and maintenance awards.

Does His Adultery Help or Hurt My Case?

In a "no-fault" state, courts will not punish a cheating spouse for causing the divorce, because it doesn't matter who is at fault. In

a "fault" divorce, allegations of adultery must be proved. Sometimes that is not easy. A *third-party witness* (a witness other
than the plaintiff or defendant) may be necessary to convince a
judge of a spouse's philandering. In the old days, women used
to hire private detectives who burst into cheating husbands'
hotel rooms and took photos, or hired female decoys to entrap
a potentially wayward spouse. With new developments in privacy laws and trespass laws, these old-fashioned techniques are
mostly outdated. Today a wife usually proves adultery with
circumstantial evidence. She must show the court circumstances
where the husband had the opportunity, motive, and intent to
have sex with another partner.

Modern-day private detectives, although costly, can
help you gather a portfolio of evidence on your husband's
activities. (In New York City, a private detective runs anywhere from one hundred to four hundred dollars an hour.)
Most private detectives are former police officers or security industry veterans. They are not the trench-coat-wearing
private eyes from the movies who follow men in broken-
down Chevys. They have sophisticated surveillance equipment, hidden cameras, and access to computerized data that
can pinpoint where people are located. They use cell phone
tracking devices that can be attached to the underside of
husbands' cars to follow their every movement. Detectives
also secretly videotape husbands dining with their mistresses
in restaurants and bars, and once in a while catch them having "dessert." Investing a thousand dollars in hiring a skilled

private eye can lead to a settlement in your favor worth much, much more.

Hit a Cheater in His Wallet

A husband's extracurricular activities can hurt his bottom line in both fault and no-fault divorces. When dividing marital property, judges in many states will take into account whether a spouse depleted marital assets during an extramarital affair and award more to the noncheating spouse. For example, some men give interest-free loans to their girlfriends, buy them expensive gifts, take them on vacation, pay for their rent, or hire them to work in their companies at unreasonably high salaries. These types of expenditures can come back to haunt a philanderer.

If the new relationship is draining his finances, a cheating husband may be forced to make financial concessions to his wife, perhaps by paying higher alimony or support. Also, if a husband spent marital money on a mistress, a wife can fight to be reimbursed in other ways at the divorce. For example, a husband who buys his girlfriend jewelry with money that also belongs to his wife can be ordered to hand over additional marital assets to offset the difference or compensate his wife in cash.

A wife has an additional remedy if her husband moves in with his girlfriend after they separate. If the mistress appears to be financially supporting him in any way, you can request a higher temporary alimony payment while the divorce is pending. If you show that she is contributing to his living expenses by paying half his rent or even supporting him, you can convince the judge that your husband's expenses are lower, so he can afford to pay you more.

Bonus Tip: You can sometimes learn information about your husband's new "roommate" from your children when they return from a visitation with their father. Kids may innocently spill the beans that a lady friend was there, or disclose how their daddy is spending his money.

What Goes Around Comes Around: How to Gather Proof of Cheating

The legal process can actually be used to gather evidence about your spouse's affair and make him very uncomfortable in the process. One way to accomplish this is by having an attorney take the deposition of your husband's mistress. Depositions are recorded sworn testimony of a witness or party that are conducted outside the courtroom. (These will be discussed in more detail in Chapter 11.) The mistress can be pulled into the divorce litigation via a deposition to help you uncover whether joint funds were used to support her.

Answers to deposition questions may help you discover details about your spouse's life that he was trying to keep secret. During one deposition I conducted on behalf of a husband, I questioned the wife's live-in boyfriend about the

minute details of their joint living arrangement: Who paid
for the electric bill, the phone bill, the food bills, restaurant
bills, their furniture, and even who paid for the gasoline for
the wife's car? I also inquired whether they slept in the same
bed and if they were affectionate in front of the children during visitation.

A deposition may serve more than one purpose. The transcript of answers provided in the deposition may be submitted
to a judge in an attempt to sway his or her position on the
terms of your divorce. Also, some wives say there is nothing
better than watching their spouse squirm when the most inti-
mate details of his love affair are revealed at the deposition table
and recorded word for word by a court stenographer.

Extra Attention Required: Taking a deposition requires
knowledge of legal rules and procedures, and a lawyer's
expertise. Be prepared to spend a decent amount of
money on legal fees.

If a wife can't afford to pay for a deposition, there is another
method of discovering evidence about a spouse's infidelity
that requires no money. You can use the tools available to you
through the legal system to gather information directly from
your husband about his conduct, spending habits, financial
status, standard of living, and more. Once your divorce is filed,
the *legal discovery* process allows you to send a list of questions

to your spouse, which he is required to answer. (For more information on the legal discovery process, see Chapter 11.)

Here's a look at a sample discovery request, provided here to give you a glimpse of the kind of information wives can seek when a husband moves in with his girlfriend while the divorce is pending. Notice how this document can help to determine how much money he is or has been spending on "the other woman" and whether that money comes from marital assets.

Jane Star v. Joe Producer
Hollywood County Superior Court
Docket number 10000000

Discovery Request:
Jane Star, the plaintiff, demands that Joe Producer, the defendant, turn over the following documents:

> *The wife wants to find out who is on the lease, who is paying his rent, or if he is paying the girlfriend's rent.*

1. A copy of the lease to the apartment where the defendant is currently residing and a list of all current occupants.

> *The wife wants to know if her soon-to-be-ex is leasing a car for his girlfriend.*

2. A copy of the lease of any vehicles the defendant is leasing.

3. A copy of the final statement of the canceled joint Visa card issued in the names of the plaintiff and the defendant.

> *The wife will learn what he was buying just before the marriage broke up.*

4. A copy of the husband's individual credit card statements over the past six months.

> *The wife is looking to determine what he has been spending marital money on. Hotels? Fancy restaurants? Vacations? Gifts for the mistress?*

5. A copy of the defendant's tennis club fee statements from the time the divorce was filed to the present.

> *Is he paying for her leisure activities?*

6. A copy of the payroll at the husband's privately owned production company.

> *The wife wants to see if the girlfriend is listed as an employee on the books.*

7. A copy of any loans or promissory notes issued by the husband in the past two years.

> *Did the husband loan his girlfriend money?*

Signed,

Jane Star

Calling His Bluff

In cases of infidelity, I have seen clients attempt to use divorce for emotional therapy, for vengeance, or to vent. A divorce should never be filed as a mechanism to seek revenge on a disloyal partner or as a wake-up call to an inattentive or disinterested partner. This plan can easily backfire. Involving the legal system will only further damage an already precarious relationship.

CHAPTER 11

Crouching Tiger, Hidden Assets: How to Find Missing Money, Assets, and Property

You will have already conducted a search for financial documents as part of your Pre-Divorce Plan. The purpose was, in part, to detect if your spouse left a paper trail leading to hidden assets or financial duplicity. Once the divorce actually begins, there are tactics you can employ to dig even deeper. Some methods are expensive and time-consuming, and require the assistance of divorce attorneys. Others are surprisingly simple, and you can do them on your own for free.

No-Cost Asset Search Techniques

Use the legal discovery process

One way to find missing property is through the legal discovery process. After a divorce action has been filed, each side is allowed to "discover" or learn facts about the other through formal written requests for information. (A deposition is also part of the legal discovery practice, but it is used to obtain oral testimony.) Any information that is relevant to the division of marital assets, child custody, child support, alimony determinations, the grounds for the divorce, or other significant matters must be disclosed to the other side when a discovery request is made. Information obtained through the discovery process can be introduced as evidence during a hearing or a trial.

Each state has its own rules about what type of evidence is discoverable and what procedure should be used to make a discovery request. Most jurisdictions allow one spouse to send the other a formal written demand for relevant documents or answers to specific questions. This is called the filing of *interrogatories* and *requests for production of documents.*

Of these two types of discovery requests, interrogatories force your spouse to answer questions, and requests for production (also called *requests for information* or *document demands*) require your spouse to produce paperwork.

Interrogatories

Interrogatories are a set of written questions that are posed to an opposing party in order to gather factual information during a lawsuit. You can send interrogatories to your husband, asking him questions relevant to your divorce action, and he is required by law to answer in writing. If your spouse tries to fight your interrogatory demand by refusing to reveal the requested information, a judge can order him to comply, as long as you can demonstrate to the court that your document search is relevant and reasonable. If he remains uncooperative, a judge may hold him in contempt of court, impose sanctions, or punish him by awarding you a larger share of the assets.

Requests for Production of Documents

Through a request for production, you can demand that your spouse deliver to you copies of documents relevant to your divorce, such as business records, receipts, his individual bank account statement, or loan documents. The court will force him to comply, even if he claims the requested information is private or personal.

Here's an example of what a request for production might look like in a divorce where the couple has significant assets and a family business called U Rent a Van. In this case, the wife's goal is to find out what her husband's business is worth through discovery.

Sample Request for Production

Jane Doe v. John Doe
Docket number FC23765/2007
Madison County Family Court

Jane Doe hereby demands that John Doe turn over the following items, which are likely to lead to the discovery of admissible evidence pertaining to the above-captioned matter:

This will uncover what the business's cash assets are.

1. All bank statements from the business U Rent a Van.

2. A copy of the accounting ledgers, books and financial statements, expense reports and disbursements from U Rent a Van.

This will tell the wife about business debts and what the business is worth.

3. A copy of the corporate tax returns filed in the past five years by U Rent a Van.

This will reveal what the business was earning before the divorce was filed.

4. A copy of any contracts for services rendered by U Rent a Van to any business, company, or corporation.

> *This will reveal what profit the business expects to earn.*

5. A copy of the payroll of U Rent a Van for the past three years.

> *This will give an idea of the size of the business and the cost of operations.*

6. A list of any outstanding customer accounts and the amount of payment owed to U Rent a Van.

Signed

Jane Doe

> *This information reveals if the business is owed money from prior transactions.*

Use your husband's prior tax returns to identify inconsistencies

During your Pre-Divorce Plan document search, you collected up to five years' worth of prior income tax returns from the marriage. Here is where these come into play. Returns may reveal inconsistencies or financial improprieties that can subtly be used as a bargaining chip during property division negotiations.

If you determine that your spouse has omitted or manipulated information over the years, you will have some additional leverage when negotiating your settlement agreement. Ostensibly, when husbands learn you are armed with this knowledge, they may decide it is smarter to settle with you than to risk the information being disclosed in open court.

Be Careful: Fraud, tax evasion, improper expense account billing, lies on loan and mortgage applications, and shady business practices can expose your husband to possible criminal charges, jail time, or a civil lawsuit. Fraudulent tax returns can also subject the filer to federal charges for lying under oath. You will need to weigh whether it's worth highlighting your spouse's illegal activity to the court. If his activities were egregious, warranting criminal charges, keep in mind that a jailed husband won't be able to work. If he is cut off from earning income, you may eventually be deprived of alimony or child support payments.

Demand an asset disclosure statement from your husband

To prove your husband's current net worth and income, collect his asset statement. This information is available because you are both required to file a *financial affidavit* (sometimes called a *disclosure of assets statement* or a *net worth statement*). Financial statements used in divorce proceedings are legal documents supported by an oath, which validates their accuracy and validity.

Many courts have written forms that parties can fill out to make their disclosures. Generally, both spouses will list the amounts in their bank accounts and locations of their financial institutions; what stocks or bonds or treasury instruments they own; the values of their 401(k) plans, individual retirement accounts or investment funds; their valuable personal possessions (art, cars, jewelry, antiques); any real estate owned individually, as well as any outstanding loans or debt.

If a party cheats or lies on the statement, it can be considered *perjury*, a criminal offense. Although lies on financial affidavits submitted in divorce court are rarely prosecuted, they *can* turn the opinion of the judge against the wrongful spouse. Yet despite the significance of this document and the parties' legal obligation to accurately and thoroughly disclose what money and property they have, some still intentionally misrepresent their net worth in an attempt to cheat their spouse out of receiving a fair share.

Keep an eye out as to whether your husband is undervaluing his wealth, hoping to give you less. I have seen many clients, upon reviewing their spouse's financial affidavits, realize that financial information was manipulated, income was missing or misrepresented, or that their husbands had underestimated the extent of their net worth.

Compare and contrast all the financial documents you collected as part of your Pre-Divorce Plan asset search (W-2s, brokerage account and bank statements, etc.) with your husband's financial affidavit, to detect if he is trying to cheat you from your share of the marital assets. If you notice omissions or inconsistencies in your spouse's financial affidavit, you may now have some leverage in your divorce negotiations. You can often convince him to "show you the money" before you show the court his questionable paperwork.

Bonus Tip: If you catch your spouse in a lie on his financial affidavit, demand that he correct his error by immediately submitting an *amended affidavit* or *updated financial affidavit*. If he continues to lie or omit information on his amended disclosure statement, you will have ammunition in front of a judge. Courts rely heavily on these documents if they are asked to determine how assets should be divided between the parties. If your husband tries to create an "unfair advantage" by revealing less than he should on his affidavit, the judge may punish him by awarding you additional assets.

Asset Search Techniques That Cost Money

It may take a bit more digging, and some funding, to find what you're looking for. Sometimes it costs money to find money. Here's how it's done:

Hire a Forensic Accountant

If your spouse has a high net worth, your dollars may be well spent on hiring a forensic accountant. These experts were introduced in Chapter 3 to help you locate missing documents and follow financial paper trails before the divorce begins. But while a divorce is pending, they can have even greater value.

Forensic accountants are experts in assembling financial documentation and examining and interpreting tax records, bank statements, share and asset transfers, credit card bills, and accounting ledgers. They can help you discover the existence of additional assets, such as a stock portfolio or a bank account that you never knew existed. They can also value family-owned businesses, which will help you get a fair share.

Time and again I have seen husbands understate the value of their business or hide business assets to prevent the wife from staking a larger claim. Even when you don't plan on seeking an ownership interest, a high-value business can be an important bargaining chip in property negotiations. Once you know what your husband's company is worth, you can demand other equally valued property or a cash equivalent in exchange for waiving your claim to it.

Forensic accountants will uncover the truth about a husband's unfair divorce tactics. The money spent on accountant fees is often made back, and then some, due to the larger settlement packages wives tend to receive as a result of their work.

Depositions

Once the divorce lawsuit has been filed, most states allow divorcing parties to conduct *depositions* of witnesses to learn information about the other side's case. Depositions are interviews of witnesses under oath that occur outside of a courtroom. Your lawyer can depose, for example, your husband, his bookkeeper, his accountant, or his secretary to learn about his financial transactions or business activities.

A deposition can cost several hundred to several thousand dollars, depending on its length. There are fees for hiring a transcriber or court stenographer, publishing the transcript (you must pay for your and your spouse's copy), and attorney billable hours for preparing and conducting the deposition. You and your lawyer will need to consider whether this strategy is likely to produce enough relevant evidence for your side of the case to make your investment worthwhile.

Out of Luck: When Hidden Money Stays Hidden

Sometimes it will be virtually impossible for you to find missing income, especially if it was in cash. If your spouse has a cash business or cash assets, there will be no paper trail leading to his assets. Since cash that has been spent can't be traced, you would be out of luck in determining your husband's true net worth.

Bonus Tip: If you are having trouble locating assets or proving that your husband is lying on his financial statements, here's where another aspect of the Pre-Divorce Plan will prove to be helpful. Present the photographs you took of your property to convince a judge that the lifestyle you lived is inconsistent with your husband's claim that he has little or no income to disclose.

Performing a successful martial asset search really strengthens your position in a divorce action. Once you can assess *and* access the financial resources available to you, you will increase your odds of winning a fair divorce settlement. With your full financial picture exposed, you can prevent your spouse from paying you less than he really should when it's time to divide your property.

CHAPTER 12
The Quickie: A Do-It-Yourself Divorce

Now that you have learned the mechanics of how a divorce action is processed, what paperwork is filed, how judges make their decisions, and what goes on behind the scenes in divorce court, you will have a better understanding of how to navigate your divorce. Depending on the particular circumstances of your own situation, you may be in a position to file a do-it-yourself divorce or personally handle the most time-consuming (lawyer translation: *expensive*) aspects of your divorce, and then use a lawyer at the end to seal the deal.

Average divorce costs run in the range of two thousand to five thousand dollars, and if issues are contested, the costs can skyrocket to tens of thousands of dollars. Divorce attorneys charge anywhere from one hundred dollars an hour in small towns to powerhouse fees of six hundred to eight hundred dollars an hour in big cities, with the national average fee around two hundred to four hundred dollars an hour. Generally, the bigger the firm you go to, the bigger the fee, with a lot of the cost going to the firm's overhead. To add insult to injury, most lawyers expect you to pay a *retainer*, or an up-front lump-sum fee, that they will bill against when they begin work on your case. Every single task a lawyer performs related to your divorce action—including answering your thirty-second phone call—will result in a bill.

For an uncomplicated divorce (e.g., uncontested, not hostile), a lawyer might not be necessary, and it's possible for you and your spouse yourselves through the legal process (though you should certainly consult with a lawyer initially if you're not sure whether a do-it-yourself divorce is appropriate for you). You can drastically cut the costs of your divorce by completing most, if not all, of the steps listed here on your own.

Do-It-Yourself Divorce Checklist

❑ *Draft Your Own Divorce Complaint or Petition*

A divorce action requires the drafting of a *complaint* or *petition*, which is a sworn document asking the court to entertain your application to dissolve the marriage. In many states, you can download a form from your court's website or pick up divorce forms from your local court clerk's office. Call ahead to see if your divorce court makes them available to the general public. Using your knowledge from Chapter 7, you can fill the forms out yourself. Sometimes they're really simple and provide boxes that can be checked off, or you can fill in the blanks.

If your jurisdiction doesn't supply legal forms, the clerk may provide literature with instructions on how to draft a divorce complaint. You can also purchase forms from a legal document preparation store.

If you are required to draft your own complaint, it must contain some crucial information, including:

- the parties' names and states of residence
- the date and location of the marriage
- the grounds for the divorce
- whether there are any minor children to the marriage
- an actual written request for the court to dissolve the marriage

Be Careful: Check with the court clerk to see if your complaint meets your state's requirements. (Chapter 7 provides additional details on the contents of a complaint.)

❏ *Complete Service of Process*

Next, hire a sheriff, constable, marshal, or licensed process server (depending on what your state law requires) to serve the legal papers on your spouse. The legal papers you will need to have served consist of a complaint or a summons, or both. A *summons* is a document that advises your spouse that his appearance is required in court and may also state the grounds for divorce. Check with your court's website or the clerk's office for the court's requirements. In most states, there is no legal effect if you personally hand your husband his walking papers. A third party must do it. Ask your local court clerk for details on how to achieve legal *service of process*.

Bonus Tip: The simplest, fastest way to make contact with a clerk is to call the courthouse where your divorce action will be filed (the local family court, divorce court, or matrimonial court) and ask to be connected to the clerk's office.

If no one will answer your questions by phone, I suggest making a trip to the courthouse to see a clerk in person. While you're there, you may be able to pick up a free pamphlet, which will guide you through the steps of filing and serving divorce papers.

Strategy Tip: I suggest that if you are going to have your husband served with papers, it's time to give him a heads-up. It's unnerving for anyone to have legal documents placed in their hands, naming them as a defendant in a lawsuit. You don't want to ambush your husband and alienate him before the divorce has even started. (You can read about my own experience having my husband served with divorce papers in Chapter 7.)

❏ *File the Divorce Papers with the Court*

Many states allow a divorce to begin when a party files the papers with the court. But which papers need to be filed and in what order depends on the rules of your local divorce court. Some states require that you file the complaint with the court before you serve it on your husband. Others allow you to file the complaint after he has been served with a summons.

Other jurisdictions require that you first serve a complaint and a summons together, and then file both documents with the court. Yet another variation is that in some states you can start a divorce by filing a summons without a complaint. So once again, it's time to check in with your local court clerk. They will be able to tell you what papers to file and the proper order to file them in.

❏ Have Your Spouse Draft His Answer to the Complaint

Once your spouse is formally served, he will be legally required to respond to the court in writing and/or in person, or risk losing the divorce lawsuit by default. Your spouse is now called the *defendant*. A defendant is required to file a legal document called an *answer*. He must answer the charges made in the divorce complaint, line by line, with one of one of the following three responses: "I agree," "I disagree," or "I don't have enough information to respond." The answers alert the court as to which issues, if any, will need to be litigated during the divorce action.

❏ Negotiate a Property Division Agreement

For the next step, you will be expected to negotiate your own property settlement agreement. You and your husband need to sit down together and decide who takes what from the marriage. Locate the marital assets before you get to the bargaining table (see Chapter 3 on how to accomplish this), so you can make an informed decision on what to accept as your share. (Read Chapter 13 to review the guidelines courts use to divide property, which will give you an idea of what legally should be yours.)

Negotiate with your spouse over who gets the car, the house, the furniture, the money, the stocks, and all other valuables and assets. Decide who is responsible for debt and financial obligations. When everything has been decided, draft a property division agreement reflecting all of your joint decisions.

A Must: Don't forget to work out who is going to pay health insurance premiums and whose policy is going to cover you, your children, and your spouse after the divorce. (See Chapter 18 for more details.) It's crucial to incorporate this decision in writing as part of your agreement.

❏ *Address Alimony, Child Support, and Visitation*

If relevant, you will also need to work out issues of spousal maintenance (a lump-sum support payment or alimony), child support, visitation, and custody. (See Chapter 16, The Support Report.)

Chapter 13 will show you the factors courts weigh to shape their alimony decisions, which will give you an idea of how a dollar value is decided. You and your spouse can follow similar guidelines to determine a fair way to structure support payments and reach an agreement on an amount. The court will decide an alimony award if you can't work it out yourselves.

The amount of alimony judges award, if any, is decided on a case-by-case basis and is tough to predict with any certainty.

To determine child support payments, each state's courts publish guidelines, which dictate the minimal amount that a noncustodial parent must pay. You can find a copy of these guidelines in your local divorce court's clerk's office.

Next, decide on which parent will have physical custody of the children (whom the children will live with), decide whether one or both parents will be authorized to make decisions on behalf of the children, and set a visitation schedule for the children to visit the noncustodial parent. Both parties must agree in writing.

Strategy Tip: If you receive alimony, you will have to pay taxes on it because it's treated as income. However, you won't be taxed if you receive a one-time lump-sum settlement payment in lieu of monthly alimony payments. (Child support payments are never taxed—see Chapter 16 for more details on this issue.)

Extra Attention Required: Child support and custody issues frequently become complicated or contentious, even if the remaining divorce issues, such as property division, are not in dispute. Sometimes family matters are litigated separately from the divorce action or require continued litigation after the divorce. It's best to seek legal counsel to handle these conflicts to ensure a reliable outcome.

❏ *Draft a Divorce Agreement*

Once spousal support, property division, and final decisions concerning the children are resolved, the final document, a *divorce agreement*, needs to be drafted. The agreement outlines everything you have agreed upon in contemplation of ending your marriage. It will attach or incorporate your property division agreement. Some courthouses have forms where you can fill in the blanks with the terms of your agreement, or you can also purchase agreement forms off the Internet.

❏ *Submit It!*

A divorce agreement must be submitted to a judge for approval. Once the court reviews your agreement and signs off, you will be granted your divorce. Submission deadlines and requirements vary from state to state. You can obtain more information on this from your local clerk's office.

In many states, you will be required to come to court and appear before a judge at a *dissolution hearing* before the divorce will be granted. At the hearing, your case will be called on the record. You and your husband will identify yourselves to the court. The judge will ask you both if there are any objections to the agreement submitted. If not, the divorce will be granted, and you will be herded out of the courtroom to make room for the next couple in line.

In other states, you won't be required to attend court. The judge will sign off on your divorce filings, and mail each of you a finalized, signed, and stamped legal document known as the *divorce decree*.

Sources of Free Information for Filing a Divorce Action in Your State

- Literature, guidebooks, handouts, or pamphlets from the clerk's office located at the divorce court or family court.
- Take a number! Get in line and speak to a clerk directly at the counter for instructions on special steps required in your state.
- Contact your county or city's local bar association to see if they offer free legal advice or assistance for filing divorce actions.
- Check your local family court or divorce court website for free downloads containing forms, instructions, and explanations on court procedures, laws, and filing requirements.

Do-It-Yourself Divorce Review

1. Draft your own divorce complaint.
2. Complete service of process.
3. File the divorce papers with the court.
4. Have your spouse draft and file his answer to the complaint.
5. Negotiate the property division agreement.
6. Address alimony, child support, custody, and visitation.
7. Draft a divorce agreement outlining the terms you negotiated.
8. Submit your final divorce agreement to the court.
9. Await the judge's signature for the divorce to be final.

CHAPTER 13

What's Mine Is Mine, What's Yours Is Mine: How Property Gets Divided in a Divorce

To get an idea of what property you should be fighting for and what you can expect to receive, you must first understand how the laws of your state affect property division. Whether you negotiate on your own or in front of a judge, what you are entitled to depends on whether you live in a *community property law* state or an *equitable distribution law* state.

As of this writing, community property law states are:

- Arizona
- California
- Idaho
- Louisiana
- Nevada
- New Mexico
- Texas
- Washington
- Wisconsin

The rest of the country follows the principles of equitable distribution law. State laws are there to guide how property should be distributed by a court, but the sky is the limit on what you can get if you can convince your husband to agree!

When Is Property Separate, and When Does It Belong to Both of Us?

Once you know what type of state law governs the division of your property, what belongs to you alone and what belongs to you and your husband together depends on how your property is classified. There are three types of classifications: *separate property, marital property*, and *community property*.

What Exactly Is Separate Property?

In both community property states and equitable distribution states, separate property is:

1. any property acquired or owned before the marriage;
2. inherited property or property received as a gift from someone other than your spouse during the marriage;
3. personal injury awards (in most states);
4. property obtained or income earned either after legal separation or after a divorce action begins (depending on your state).

Extra Attention Required: Categorizing property obtained by either spouse once a divorce is underway presents a complicated legal issue with several variables. The first issue is whether the state where your divorce action is filed considers property to be separate based on the separation date or on the date the divorce action is commenced. Once that rule is known, the next issue is determining what date constitutes the legal separation date or what date is considered the start of a divorce action. If couples don't agree, litigation may be necessary to reach a conclusion.

In many states, the date a couple separates is open to debate. If necessary, spouses will try to convince a court what date it should recognize by presenting evidence, such as that one spouse moved out. Also, different states' laws define the date when a divorce action begins differently. Some consider it to be the date the divorce papers were served, others consider the date of filing, and still others recognize the date a case is assigned an index or docket number with the court.

Because separate property is considered "separate" from the marriage, it won't be divided in a divorce. Separate property is returned to the spouse who brought it into the marriage.

What Exactly Is Marital Property?

Marital property is any property accumulated from the date of the marriage until a divorce action is commenced (again, this date is determined differently from state to state), except for inheritances, gifts from third parties, and most personal injury awards. In equitable distribution states, both you and your husband equally own marital property while married, but it is not necessarily divided equally in a divorce. One spouse may be entitled to a greater share of marital property than the other. Some examples of marital property are:

- A house purchased with joint funds (or with separate funds when it is titled in both spouses' names)
- Salary earned by either spouse during the marriage
- Gifts between spouses
- The family car

And Finally, What Exactly Is Community Property?

Community property only exists in community property law states. It is property belonging to the marriage—what most people would commonly think of as marital property—except that the term "marital property" does not apply in a community property state.

Community property is any property acquired or income earned during a marriage by the labor of either party, excluding separate property, such as inheritances, gifts from third parties, and most personal injury awards. Any property purchased during the marriage from community funds (or from separate funds if the item is a gift to the marriage) is community property. Community property is owned equally by both spouses during the marriage and divided equally in a divorce.

Although there are a number of differences in the laws of individual community property law states, they all operate under the same principle. Each spouse contributes equally to a marriage, so each spouse is entitled to an equal share of the community property.

Some examples of community property are:

- Artwork purchased on the couple's honeymoon
- Interest from a joint bank account
- Salary earned by either spouse during the marriage
- An Internet business started by both spouses but managed by the husband
- Rent from a separate apartment attached to a couple's home

Once property is classified as separate, marital, or community, each spouse's share will be determined based on whether community property guidelines or equitable distribution guidelines apply.

What Is Equitable Distribution?

In an equitable distribution state, marital property gets divided based on what's "fair." There is no rule for an even split or any other mathematical formula. Marital assets are distributed "fairly and equitably" and with some flexibility, depending on the parties' unique personal circumstances.

If a couple allows a court to divide their property, a judge will weigh and balance many factors, including:

- the length of the marriage
- the earning capacity of both spouses
- the health or special needs of the parties or the children
- the couple's standard of living

If spouses decide, however, to distribute marital property on their own and without court assistance, they can do whatever they want. (See Chapter 15 on do-it-yourself property division.) The only barrier is if there's an enforceable *prenuptial agreement* in effect. Prenuptial agreements are a wealthy spouse's best remedy to keep certain assets away from a soon-to-be-ex. Spouses who sign away their rights to property in a valid pre-divorce contract are going to have a hard time voiding that promise in divorce court, although it's not impossible!

Now, let us take a closer look at what factors courts examine when deciding how to distribute property "equitably" between spouses.

1. Contribution to the marriage

An asset may be divided based on who earned the money to buy it, the contribution of a homemaker spouse that enabled the working spouse to earn income to buy it, and whether the asset was bought with money earned before or during the marriage.

2. Value of the property

To divide property fairly, courts consider its value. Timing is the key issue here. Courts measure the value of property either at the time the divorce is initiated or when the couple separates, depending on your state. Timing is significant for assets like stocks or real estate, which can easily fluctuate in value from the time a couple splits up until the divorce is finalized.

3. The length of the marriage

In an equitable distribution state, don't expect a big payout if you were only in the game a short time. A one- to three-year marriage would certainly be considered short. But believe it or not, some states consider five years, seven years, or even ten years to be a short marriage. Usually, the shorter the marriage, the smaller the property division award. That's because judges won't award much to a wife who hasn't been married long enough to contribute to the growth of marital assets. (I have seen some truly short-term brides walk away with only the clothes on their backs and their wedding ring.)

4. The future

Courts will weigh the probable future economic circumstance of the parties: Will a spouse be unable to work due to age or infirmity? Does a nonworking spouse have sufficient skills to get a job, and at what pay scale?

5. The amount of income of each spouse and the sources of that income

The judge will consider how much money is in the marital pot, who earned it, and whether there is income that came from a gift or inheritance and is not subject to division.

6. Inheritance rights and benefit rights

Judges will examine the potential loss of inheritance rights or pension rights to the spouse who didn't own them, but was benefiting from them during the marriage.

7. The quantity and quality of marital property available to divide

Judges will balance the equity and fairness of awarding both alimony and property. For example, if a wife gets a higher alimony award, she may get a smaller property award and vice versa.

8. Asset liquidity

What assets are available and are they *liquid*? Can the property be divided now or only upon its sale in the future?

9. The practicality of splitting the assets

Is there a business asset, for example, that is going to be hard to divide? If so, what other property is available to the spouse who doesn't run the business?

Your Bottom Line

It's hard to predict how a judge will decide property awards under equitable distribution. Not only do the results vary from state to state, but there is no uniformity among decisions within the states, since each judge handling a divorce case gets to dictate what he or she thinks is fair. Fairness is always open to interpretation, therefore results can even differ from couple to couple within the same courthouse.

How Do Community Property Laws Affect Property Division?

Community property law is more predictable than equitable distribution law, because each spouse is entitled to a one-half share of community property. This is known as the fifty-fifty rule. The theory is that any property owned by the "marital community" belongs to both parties equally.

In a community property state, courts scrutinize all the financial activity that occurs from the time the couple is married until they separate or initiate divorce. Almost all assets acquired during the marriage, with a few exceptions, exist as "community property" and are subject to a fifty-fifty split (unless there's a prenuptial agreement specifying a different division).

Occasionally, courts will disregard the fifty-fifty split rule and order a different distribution in "the interests of fairness and justice." For example, if there is a special-needs child in the house, the court may order additional maintenance for the caregiving parent or they may direct that the spouse be allowed to stay in the home with the child. Special accommodations may also be made when a spouse is disabled and has an impaired earning capacity. The court may order the healthy spouse to provide extra resources to benefit the disadvantaged partner.

Extra Attention Required: Some types of community property are more difficult to divide. These are special assets that are earned during the marriage, but vest at a future date, such as retirement benefits, employee bonuses, pension plans, and stock options. Assets purchased with separate funds and community property funds combined also fall into this category. They are divided by a more complicated formula, so you should seek professional advice either from your attorney or a financial analyst.

Is There Any Advantage to Getting Divorced in a Community Property State?

In community property states, regardless of how briefly a union lasted, if a marriage acquires assets or the husband earns a big income, wives generally get better financial settlements than in equitable distribution states because of the fifty-fifty rule. Hollywood wives in particular have reaped enormous divorce settlements thanks to community property laws, coupled with their husbands' substantial income and assets. (Remember, California is a community property state.)

Actor Michael Douglas's ex-wife Diandra walked away with an estimated forty-five to sixty million dollars from a twenty-three-year marriage. Actress Amy Irving reportedly netted a windfall of one hundred million dollars in her divorce from director Steven Spielberg after a four-year marriage that produced one child.

You don't have to be mega-rich or married for decades to

do well in a community property state divorce. Sometimes the success of your property settlement can depend on luck and timing. For example, if you are married for just one year, and in that year your husband wins the lottery, triples his salary, and buys a vacation home, you are usually entitled to half of all these assets. That's not bad for a year's worth of "work."

Can you solve this community property math problem?

A woman named Lucy marries Desi in Las Vegas, Nevada (a community property state). Desi is an unemployed actor and singer with a small savings account that's running on empty. One month later, out of the blue, Desi is offered a movie part and a two-million-dollar contract where he is paid up front whether he completes the project or not.

Desi takes the job and now spends all his time at the studio, carrying on an affair with a young production assistant. Lucy finds out and divorces him one month later. From a two-month marriage, with no prenuptial agreement, how much can Lucy get?

The answer: A staggering one million dollars, or exactly one-half.

How "When It's Over" Determines What You Get Once It's Over

When the marital relationship ends is an important additional factor in determining whether a property will be considered separate or marital (or community) property. You are only entitled to receive property that was acquired or purchased while the marriage "existed."

The cutoff date when a marriage is officially over varies from state to state. Some states consider:

- The date of your *legal* separation
- The date of your *physical* separation (when the parties move out and intend not to continue the marriage)
- The date your case is assigned a file, docket, or index number in the courthouse
- The date a judge grants the divorce
- The date when the divorce trial begins
- The date the judge handling your case selects at his or her discretion
- The date the divorce papers are filed

Depending on which time frame benefits them the most, spouses often bicker over which date the court should recognize as the cutoff date to affect the results of property division. One spouse will be able to claim a greater share of the assets, and the other spouse will be forced to give more away.

CHAPTER 14
To Have and to Hold On to:
Which Assets Are Yours to Keep
After a Divorce

Who Gets What?

Many of my friends facing the prospect of divorce call me and ask how much they are going to get if their marriage is dissolved. I warn them that there's no exact science to alimony and property division, and every case can turn out differently. However, they can expect that any item brought to the marriage by one spouse as separate property will still belong to that person, and most items purchased with marital money during the marriage will be divided by a court based on the principles of equitable distribution law or community property law, depending on the state where their divorce is filed.

While each state's property division laws *suggest* which assets should be coming your way and how much you'll receive, the laws have many exceptions and loopholes that can affect (or eliminate) a spouse's entitlement to certain assets. And if there's a valid prenuptial agreement in effect, that document may dictate how all the property gets divided.

Bonus Tip: But remember, a prenup does not have to be abided by if you can convince your husband to ignore it, or negotiate your way around it.

Let the Games Begin

Now that you are ready to start divvying up your property, it's time to learn the answers to all of your asset division questions. Who gets the car? The house? The furniture? The family dog? Plus, what items can you block your husband from ever getting his hands on? And how you can prevent him from accessing legal loopholes that cut you off from your share?

What follows is an overview that demonstrates how different possessions, properties, and assets typically get distributed in a divorce. Keep in mind that if you and your husband are creative and decide to reach an agreement without court intervention, you can divide your property any way you want!

Furniture, Collectibles, Antiques, and Bric-a-Brac

Unless they are excluded by a prenup, personal possessions should be divided any way you both think is fair. If you can't agree, and your husband decides to fight you over *replaceable* personal possessions, it's almost always best to let them go. Bickering over pool tables or wine glasses wastes precious time and can delay your divorce.

Most personal effects have little value in a divorce action. Judges will look at items' actual value, not replacement value.

Since the resale value of used furniture, rugs, pots and pans, televisions, computers, and the like is often equivalent to garage-sale prices, it may not be worth your energy battling to keep them. Don't deplete your negotiation stamina or waste your emotional capital by fighting over the small stuff. Learning when to walk away from replaceable possessions will help you succeed, as well as keep your dignity, during property distribution negotiations.

Inheritances

In most states, money or assets you receive as part of an inheritance are yours and yours alone, even if received during the marriage. Since inheritances are considered separate property, you do not have to turn over any portion of an inheritance to your husband in a divorce. (A few states' judges may stray from this rule and award a portion of an inheritance to the other spouse in cases where there are no other assets available.)

However, sometimes there are other loopholes when claims are made for a portion of a spouse's inheritance. In some states, if you receive money through a will and you combine or "commingle" the money with already existing marital assets (such as depositing inheritance money in a joint bank account), your inheritance may become part of marital property. If so, your spouse would be entitled to a share of your inherited money.

Here's an example of how that can happen: If you and your husband purchase a condo for cash with thirty thousand dollars from your inheritance and sixty thousand dollars from the sale of your marital stock portfolio, and you subsequently divorce, you could lose the right to recover the full amount of your investment (thirty thousand dollars) that came from your inheritance.

Assume the condo is sold for what you paid for it, or ninety thousand dollars. Your husband can claim that your investment in the condo with proceeds from *separate property* (the inheritance) was a "gift to the marriage," and has therefore converted to *marital property*. He would further argue that half of the ninety thousand dollars invested should be his, so he deserves to receive forty-five thousand dollars from the proceeds of the condo sale.

Extra Attention Required: The "commingling" of marital and separate property presents complex legal issues. If you own property or possessions purchased with commingled money, it is best to seek professional legal advice on how to recover the full value of your inheritance or gift upon divorce.

You would likely disagree. You would want to convince a judge that the portion of the investment that came from your inheritance is separate property and should be returned to you in full. To protect your inheritance you might argue that you had no intention of gifting the portion of the condo paid for with separate funds to your husband, and that he was merely enjoying use of the property as an unequal co-owner. Therefore, after the separate inheritance money of thirty thousand dollars is deducted from the sale amount of ninety thousand dollars, your husband should only be entitled to half of what's left. Half of sixty thousand dollars (the amount invested from marital funds) is thirty thousand dollars, and that is all he should get.

Whether you will win this round depends on how your state divorce law treats the commingling of property, and how well you have convinced the judge of the merits of your position.

Gifts

If a gift, such as a car or a cottage, is given to you by someone other than your husband, he can't claim it as half his during a divorce. The majority of states consider gifts from third parties to be individual or separate property. A gift, no matter when received, will continue to be owned by you alone after a divorce.

"Commingling" issues arise if you sell your gift and combine the sale proceeds with marital property to buy something of greater value. For example, let's say that after you are married your uncle gives you a brand-new Honda Accord, titled in your name alone. You sell the Accord, and then you and your husband add twenty thousand dollars from marital funds to the proceeds and buy a Cadillac. Essentially you have commingled separate property (the Accord) with marital property (the money).

Depending on what state you live in, your husband may successfully claim that the new car is half his. His position would be that the nature of your uncle's gift changed from separate property to marital or community property, entitling him to a share. If you disagree, a judge may need to decide which part of the car is "separate." The court will weigh whether the funds from the car should be traced back to your gift and returned to you, or whether you gave your husband an ownership interest in part of your gift when you converted it into a new set of wheels.

Houses and Real Estate

Who gets to keep the family home after a divorce?

If a wife is awarded exclusive temporary residence in the house during the divorce because she cares for the children, some judges will be reluctant to interrupt the status quo and will award her the house in the divorce. However, because the carrying costs are usually high for one spouse to handle alone, many couples end up dividing their real estate. A common practice is for one spouse to buy the other out with cash or new financing, or for one spouse to give the other equally valued assets in exchange for full ownership. But when there's not enough money to go around, the house may have to be sold and the proceeds divided.

Be Careful: If you decide you want the marital home as part of your divorce settlement, make sure that you can afford it. A residence is a major expense, encompassing mortgage payments, utility costs, property taxes, insurance, repairs, and maintenance.

If you plan on selling the house and cashing out after the divorce, you will need a large enough budget to cover carrying costs until you find a suitable buyer. Don't bite off more than you can chew, because it's likely you will have less cash flow once you are on your own.

Bonus Tip: If you are determined to stay in the house, but don't have the money to run it, you might want to work out a deal with your husband where you both hold joint title to the property, and he chips in on the carrying costs. Then, when a specified date arrives (such as when the kids are no longer in school), the home can be sold and the proceeds divided.

Before you strike a deal to accept the house as a property award in lieu of other assets or in exchange for your husband receiving alternative marital property, calculate how much the sale of your house actually puts in your pocket to make sure you are getting a fair deal. There are several costs, fees, and taxes that will reduce your net sale proceeds:

1. Real estate broker's fees

   Brokers are usually paid commission in the amount of 5 to 6 percent of the sale price by you, the seller. Therefore, your sale profits will be reduced after the broker is paid.

2. Capital gains: the federal tax

   Capital gains taxes are taxes on the gain in value of your property from the time you purchased it. If there has been a significant increase in the value of your home since the time you purchased it, you may owe Uncle Sam a portion of the profit when you sell.

   However, since 1997, the capital gains laws have been extremely favorable to married couples. Under the current laws, married couples filing joint tax returns who have resided in their primary residence for at least two of the past five years do not have to pay capital gains taxes on up to $500,000 in profit from the sale of their home. So if your home sells for less than that amount, or the house appreciates up to that amount, then your gain is tax-free. Single people or married taxpayers filing separate returns are exempt from paying taxes on up to $250,000 in gain.

Several events must be carefully planned and timed with the assistance of an attorney and/or tax advisor to achieve the best possible tax advantages, such as:

- When the house is sold
- Which spouse moved out before the sale
- How the ownership interest is transferred between spouses
- Which spouse owns the house at the time of the sale
- What language is placed in the divorce agreement regarding the transfer of the house

Tax laws are difficult to navigate and subject to change. Whether the sale of your real estate is subject to capital gains tax depends on the particulars of your individual circumstances. Discuss any real estate sale or potential sale and the timing of your sale with an accountant or attorney to learn exactly what tax consequences you may face.

Be Careful: The timing of the sale of your house can have significant tax implications, particularly if you are awarded full ownership after the divorce. Depending on when you sell, you may fall into a single tax filer status for purposes of the capital gains exemption, and only be entitled to exclude up to $250,000 in gain. If so, you would not be permitted to take advantage of the higher married couple's exemption.

Bonus Tip: If a husband sells or transfers his share of the house to his wife, no taxes are owed for the transfer, even if the house has appreciated in value. But the transfer must be made during the marriage or as an "incident to a divorce." To make sure the transfer is considered incident to a divorce, it must be specifically spelled out in the divorce or separation agreement or it must occur within a specified period of time after the date the marriage ends to satisfy IRS requirements.

3. Closing costs

   Selling a home may result in two to three thousand dollars in costs and attorney's fees at closing.

4. Property taxes or transfer taxes: the state taxes

   Some states charge the seller a mandatory "transfer tax" or "conveyance tax" for the sale of real property. The tax is calculated as a percentage of the total sale price and is collected upon completion of the sale. Since these transfer taxes may be due at the time of your closing, you will likely pay them out of the proceeds of your sale.

5. State capital gains taxes

   Many states charge a capital gains tax on profit from the sale of real estate. Tax rates vary across the country. Some states tax the gain at their general personal income tax rate. Others provide exemptions from the tax similar to the federal tax laws.

6. Lack of equity

   You can't profit from a property unless there's equity. Equity in a home is the value left over after the mortgage is paid off and all loans are satisfied. In a property settlement negotiation, don't overvalue what your home is worth by failing to account for the portion that is owned by the bank or lender, and whether there has been a reduction in your home's value due to depreciation.

7. Other miscellaneous expenses

   Remember to factor in the following additional costs, fees, and expenses, which can further reduce the amount of your sale profit:

   • Land record filing fees (a few hundred dollars)
   • Attorney's fees at closing (several hundred to a few thousand dollars)
   • Fees to the title closer, depending on your county or jurisdiction (up to two hundred dollars)
   • Mortgage closing (termination) fees to the lender (several hundred to a few thousand dollars, depending on your financing)

Be Careful: Beware of "interest only" loans or mortgages. If you and your spouse secured this type of loan for your property, there may have been little to no opportunity to build additional equity by paying off the mortgage. "Interest only" loans force the borrower to pay off only the interest on the loan with no reduction in principal. Unless you have overpaid your mortgage each year, when you sell the house (even if it is twenty years later) you will owe the bank the same amount you initially borrowed. Your equity will only come from any appreciation in value of the house from the time you bought it until you sold it, but not from mortgage payments.

What if I want to keep the house and my husband claims the house is worth more/less than its true value?

You and your husband can agree together on what your house is worth and share in the equity. But if one spouse is going to buy out the other's share in the property and you can't agree on value, the best way to determine a fair price is to hire an independent, neutral appraiser. The appraiser will provide an expert opinion on the fair market value of your property.

What if my name isn't on the title?

If the court considers the house to be marital property or community property, you are entitled to a share in the equity in equitable distribution states, and half its value in community property states, regardless of whose name is on the title.

(See Chapter 13 for a review of community property law and equitable distribution law principles.)

 Be Careful: The results may be different in Mississippi and a few other states that use an old-fashioned rule, which bases property division in divorce on who holds the legal title.

However, in equitable distribution states, don't expect to get the house if the marriage lasted only a short time and it was purchased with separate property funds. If, for example, your husband put up all the money to purchase it and you were married for only a year, then regardless of whose name is on the title, a court may award the house exclusively to him. That's because it wouldn't be "equitable" to award a share of such a valuable asset to a short-term bride, who had little time to contribute financially to the marriage.

Retirement benefits/pension plans/401(k)s:

Important questions arise when it comes time to divide future benefits such as pension plans, 401(k)s, or individual retirement accounts (IRAs):

Will each spouse keep his or her own benefits?

When do the benefits vest (change from a future benefit to a present benefit)?

Should we look at present-day value or future value when dividing future benefits in a divorce?

In most cases, the portion of a retirement plan or other deferred employment benefit that was acquired during the marriage is subject to division in divorce. Many courts use a formula to calculate how to divide this asset, valuing the future benefit as if the employee were to leave the company today.

Dividing deferred compensation and benefits is tricky. The spouse who expects to receive the benefit will argue that it is "future income," and since it hasn't been earned yet, the other spouse is not entitled to a marital share. Conversely, the nonbreadwinner spouse will argue that she is entitled to a portion (or to half, in community property states) of deferred compensation because the right to receive the income was acquired during the marriage. Her position will be that even if the husband won't receive the income until the future, the right to the income was earned in the present. Therefore, it's marital property and subject to division. Who wins the argument depends on whether you are in a community property state or an equitable distribution state.

How Is a Retirement Account or 401(k) Divided?

You can divide the savings in a retirement account with your husband in several ways:

- By taking a one-time payout
- By receiving monthly payments when your husband retires
- By having a lump sum transferred into your own retirement account

Be Careful: Watch out for tax consequences with these types of transactions. Keep in mind that liquidating a retirement plan, IRA, or 401(k) before a certain age (normally fifty-nine and a half) can result in tax penalties for early withdrawal. In order to divide this tax-impacted investment, a lawyer will need to petition the court to issue a *qualified domestic relations order (QDRO)*. A QDRO will prevent tax penalties from being imposed for withdrawing money from these accounts in a divorce.

Extra Attention Required: Expert assistance from a lawyer is required if there are significant pension, 401(k), or retirement benefits. Division issues are complex, and QDRO orders must comply with a number of specific rules. Also, experts are needed to calculate when these interests vest and what they are worth at the time of divorce. The formulas for apportioning deferred compensation between spouses vary depending on your state's divorce laws.

Business Interests and Business Assets

Being a homemaker can pay off when there's a divorce. A wife may be compensated by a divorce court for providing her husband with the opportunity to lend his energy and efforts to the workplace. In most states, if you supported your husband by running the household and raising the children while he built a business or earned a degree, you may be entitled to a share in his business, practice, or company. Even entertaining your husband's business associates or running his errands while he is at work has value in the eyes of the law.

Who Gets the Business?

When a business is a couple's biggest asset, their divorce often includes a complex negotiation over who gets the company. Hypothetically, if a husband starts a business with ten thousand dollars of his own money (separate property), and after he marries the business value increases to one hundred thousand dollars, the wife can claim she is entitled to forty-five thousand dollars in equity (half the value of the increase in equity of ninety thousand dollars). The husband may rebut her claim by arguing that she is entitled to nothing because his efforts, networking, specialized skills, and business connections caused the business to grow, and she didn't contribute to the company's profitability. Which way a court decides depends on whether the couple filed their divorce in an equitable distribution law state or a community property law state, as well as how a judge might subjectively view the value of each spouse's contribution to the growth of the business.

How to Value a Business for Purposes of Property Division

Valuing a family business for purposes of property division is not a simple proposition. It requires measuring business assets against debts. If you and your spouse own a profitable or potentially valuable business, it is best to seek a professional evaluation of what it's worth. The price of an expert evaluation is usually steep, running in the thousands of dollars, but to determine your fair share of a business interest you need to know its true value. Your money will be well spent.

Disputes often arise over the value of a family business

after spouses exchange financial affidavits or net worth statements. The spouse who owns the business is required to list the company's net worth in the statement. It's often the case that the spouse who operates the business has a far different "idea" of what that asset is worth than the nonworking spouse. Read between the lines: The lower the value of the company, the smaller the stake that has to be given away in the divorce.

For example, if a husband discloses in his statement that his business is worth four hundred thousand dollars, and the wife has reason to believe the business is worth seven hundred thousand dollars, she should immediately hire a forensic accountant. She will need an expert to inspect the books, follow accounting paper trails, view the premises, and tally inventory to determine how much the business is worth. If a husband disputes his wife's expert's findings, he can get his own appraisal. Then the couple would submit their reports to a judge and litigate the issue, until a court rules which value will be deemed official for purposes of asset division.

How Couples Can Divide a Family Business

For family businesses of modest value, there are some simple and inexpensive options if you decide to handle the division of this asset on your own.

Option 1: A buyout

One spouse keeps the business, and then gives the other spouse a cash equivalent.

Why this option works: The business entity remains intact after a divorce, and there are no costs incurred (filing fees, attorneys' fees) by avoiding a potential change in the corporate structure.

Potential problem: Many times, when a spouse owns his or her own business, the company constitutes most or all of that spouse's entire net worth. There often aren't enough additional marital assets of equal value to compensate the nonworking spouse.

Option 2: Sell the business and split the proceeds

Sell the business to a third party and divide the profits.

Why this option works: This move liquidates the asset, allowing for a simple division of equity.

Potential problem: If you want to resolve all your financial issues quickly, you may run into a roadblock. You can't predict whether you will get the right buyer at the right time to pay the right price.

Option 3: Structure ownership in the business at fifty-fifty, or some other split that is fair to both spouses

Fairly divide the business.

Why this option works: If the business is the main family asset and there isn't much other property to be divided, this allows the business to continue operations and provide income to the spouses.

Potential problem: If both spouses decide to keep an ownership interest, they will be forced to maintain a business relationship long after their marital relationship ends. If personalities continue to clash, this arrangement might preclude a successful "working environment."

Option 4: Keep ownership at status quo and compensate the nonowner spouse

The owner will keep the business and compensate the nonowner with a higher maintenance or alimony award, or property award.

Why this option works: The business entity remains intact after a divorce, and there are no costs incurred (filing fees, attorneys' fees) by avoiding a potential change in the corporate structure.

Potential problem: If a wife accepts a higher alimony payment as compensation in exchange for the company, she should keep in mind that she will be paying taxes on that money as if it's income. She needs to make accurate "after-tax" calculations of the true value of her alimony package to determine if she would be getting a fair deal.

If a Couple Can't Agree, Here's How Courts
May Divide a Family Business

Often a business asset is so valuable or financially complex that couples are unable to succeed with do-it-yourself business asset division. In that case, the battle moves to the courtroom, where it is the judge who will decide a fair apportionment. Courts may look at the following factors before splitting up a business asset between spouses:

- Did one spouse come to the marriage with an already profitable and operational business? If so, the other spouse may or may not be entitled to a share.
- Did one spouse come to the marriage with an already profitable and operational business, but through his labor during the marriage, did the business increase in profitability? If so, the other spouse may be entitled to a share.
- Did the nonworking spouse contribute to the business's increased value? If so, he or she may be entitled to a share.
- Was the working spouse the sole contributor to the increase in value of the business? If so, the other spouse may not be entitled to a share, unless she can argue that her homemaker duties aided the husband's ability to grow the business.

Bank Accounts

Joint bank accounts (accounts held in both spouse's names) are presumed to be owned equally. Therefore they are usually divided equally in a divorce. Individual accounts are considered individual or separate property. But if a spouse uses an individual account to improperly stash marital funds, you are entitled to a share of that money.

Pets

A pet, under the law, is a possession, regardless of whether you consider it a member of your family. You obviously can't divide your pet in a divorce, but you can share custody. Some couples arrange for joint pet custody as part of their divorce agreement, even working out visitation schedules by shifting the animal to different houses during different days of the week. I have seen some parties draft clauses making one spouse responsible for vet bills if the animal gets sick on their visitation shift.

Bonus Tip: Since pets are considered personal property, if your pet custody agreement is incorporated into your divorce settlement agreement, you can have a judge enforce the terms of your deal if your spouse later violates it.

Stocks, Mutual Funds, Bonds, and Stock Portfolios

As part of a divorce settlement, the transfer between spouses of monetary assets (ie., stocks and bonds) and real estate is not taxable. So, for example, if a spouse gets the stock portfolio, there will be no taxes assessed unless and until the asset is sold to a third party.

Extra Attention Required: If you plan on liquidating marital assets by selling them to a third party, check with an attorney, accountant, or financial adviser to confirm what, if any, tax implications there will be and when the best time is to sell.

Professional Degrees

In many states, a business, medical, or law degree is considered a marital asset and its value is subject to distribution. Some states will award a wife a percentage of the value of her husband's degree because it comes with a "future income stream." In states where a professional degree is not treated as marital property, courts will only consider awarding a wife a share in her husband's increased *earning capacity* as a result of the degree, rather than awarding her a share in the value of the degree itself. Consult with a local attorney for the law that applies in your state.

Your Last Will and Testament

You may be surprised to learn that inheritance provisions in a spouse's last will and testament can be subject to divorce negotiations. Wives can bargain over what promises or property bequests their soon-to-be-ex-husbands will write into their wills. Although negotiating the content of a will is often overlooked during property and asset division, achieving an agreement cannot only benefit a spouse, but can also protect the children in certain circumstances.

For example, if there are few marital assets, but a husband is expected to inherit from wealthy family members, a wife would be wise to secure a future stake in that interest. She can accomplish this by seeking a guarantee that her husband will make a specific bequest in his will governing how his property or assets will be disposed of. This is known as a future interest in an estate. A future interest has no present value, but will become valuable at a future date—in this case, the date of her husband's death.

Sometimes the following will provisions are negotiated as part of a property settlement agreement:

- Your husband must bequeath money or a percentage of his estate to you, or if you die before him, to the children.
- Your husband must bequeath money directly to the children.
- You both must bequeath money to each other.

Getting a will "guarantee" from your husband during a divorce serves well to protect your children in the event he remarries. There have been many unfortunate cases where an ex-husband, either intentionally or unintentionally, leaves all his money to his new wife, and the children inherit nothing. Even if a father expected the next wife to "take care" of his children from an earlier marriage upon his death, she would be under no financial obligation to do so. I personally know several children from different families who were omitted from a parent's will after a second marriage. They didn't receive a penny from their fathers' estates, because their stepmothers refused to share their inheritances. One friend sadly commented, "Because of his oversight, all my father's hard-earned money went to a woman we barely know."

If you include a provision in your divorce agreement directing how your husband will dispose of his estate, it will not be enforceable until after his death. A will is not a legally enforceable instrument until the *testator* (person who makes a will) dies. But even then, getting what was promised may not necessarily be a simple proposition.

A testator may change his will at any time while he is alive. If your ex-husband violates your divorce agreement by eliminating the promised provision (or failing to add it), you will have to wait for his estate to be set up after his death to enforce the terms of the divorce contract. Your recourse would be to sue his estate to recover the inheritance you or the children were promised.

Be Careful: Divorce agreements governing inheritance issues involve a complex overlap of estate law and divorce law. It is often a costly and time-consuming process to sue an estate in Probate Court to enforce a divorce agreement. Seek professional legal advice and counsel if you are pursuing these interests.

Alternative and Creative Property Distribution

There's no rule in divorce that says you are limited to dividing only the marital assets from your property inventory list. Depending on your husband's wealth and financial resources, you can get creative. Why not negotiate for your spouse to foot the bill for various facets of your post-divorce lifestyle in exchange for you giving him something he values? Here are some unconventional items that have been negotiated into settlement agreements:

- Health club membership fees
- Free services or products from a husband's business or company
- A job and salary from a husband's business or company

- Payment of your mental health and therapy bills
- Continued use of "family and friends" discounts and promotional opportunities from the husband's employer
- Frequent flier miles
- Payment of plastic surgery bills (nose jobs, liposuction, facelifts, or BOTOX treatments)

Property Division Advice

If you unnecessarily provoke your spouse, you risk losing your leverage at the bargaining table. Don't go after property, particularly personal possessions, that have sentimental value to your husband.

****

Take It From Someone Who Knows: My husband owned a ski boat, which he cherished. I could have asked him for half its value. I knew that psychologically that would have been a bad move. He would have gotten defensive and shut down communications if he believed I was trying to "take part of his boat." Instead I asked him for an alternative asset equal in value to my share.

****

Demanding assets out of spite or vengeance sets a bad tone and can hamper your husband's future cooperation. It might encourage him to go after the things that have sentimental value to you. This can be very harmful when you need to ask for additional concessions later in the divorce process. A man is not likely to give you what you want, if you push his buttons the wrong way.

CHAPTER 15
Divide and Conquer:
A Beginner's Guide to Do-It-Yourself
Property Division

Marriage is essentially a business relationship between two people, with love as part of the equation. In any business, when partners close up shop and go their separate ways, they need to decide how the assets of the business will be divided. It's the same in a divorce. Before a marriage can be legally terminated, a couple must negotiate how everything purchased, saved, or received during the relationship will be distributed between them. The final step is to draft a property settlement agreement spelling out their decisions.

Save Money by Doing It Yourself

The distribution and division of money, assets, and property is usually a time-consuming and expensive part of a divorce action. If a lawyer is handling your divorce and marital assets are not complex, my advice is to handle this task yourself to cut divorce costs. Under certain circumstances, paying lawyers to accomplish this for you is like throwing money down the drain.

The bickering that occurs over asset division has always been a tremendous source of income for the legal profession. The key moneymakers for the lawyers are the clients who pay them to handle what I call "pots and pans" arguments. These are fights over nonessential items of personal property, from pots and pans to Persian rugs to pool tables. I have seen attorneys do minimal work and generate enormous bills during the property division phase of a divorce, because couples didn't know or didn't want to handle splitting up their possessions on their own.

With lawyers involved, battles over "stuff" can cost you a fortune. After one of my clients moved out of the family home, he paid me to make several phone calls and send a letter to his wife's attorney requesting the return of his seventy-five-dollar George Foreman grill. I unsuccessfully reasoned with him that it would cost him nothing to pick up the phone and call his wife directly, or that he should buy a new grill, rather than spend money on legal fees to get it back. But because communications with his spouse had broken down completely, the only way the couple would interact was through their attorneys.

Why does it cost so much for lawyers to get involved? Here's a step-by-step overview of how an attorney's bill is generated when the task of dividing personal property is at hand. Notice how a small task can very quickly turn into a large legal bill.

1. To begin, the attorney takes the client's call to listen to her property division request: "Tell my husband I want the silverware." (The phone call is *billable time*.)

2. Next, the wife's attorney calls the husband's attorney to tell him or her, "My client wants the silverware." *(Billable time.)*

3. That attorney will then call his client, the husband, and convey the wife's "position." *(Billable time* for the opposing counsel.)

4. Then the wife's attorney will wait for opposing counsel to call them back. The two lawyers may engage in telephone tag until they connect. Every time the wife's attorney picks up the phone to call the other side, it costs the client money, even if the call goes to voice mail. *(Billable time.)*

5. The lawyers finally speak on the telephone. They negotiate over who should get the silverware. *(Billable time.)*

6. The husband's counsel may need to call his client back with more information from the phone call: "Hey, your wife is really serious about this silverware. Do you want to give it to her?" *(Billable time* for the opposing counsel.)

7. Once the husband's counsel gets back to the wife's attorney with the husband's position, the wife's attorney will then call her back and tell her the outcome of the discussion. *(Billable time.)*

8. If the lawyers couldn't resolve the issue and the wife wants to press forward, her attorney may discuss the possibility of court action with her, such as filing a motion asking the

judge to order the return of the silverware. This explanation takes up time and will result in a bill. *(Billable time.)*

9. To protect the wife, her attorney may send "legal correspondence" (a letter) to opposing counsel summarizing the outcome of the discussions, like this one:

Dear Opposing Counsel,

To confirm our telephone conversation of today's date, it is my understanding that your client will turn over the silverware to my client on the first day of the month. Thank you for your attention to this matter. Very truly yours.

(Billable time.)

Was it worth it? This client just accrued attorney billable time at the rate of three hundred to four hundred dollars an hour to net some silverware. I hope it was genuine silver. The opposing spouse probably spent close to the same on his lawyer. A telephone call or e-mail from one spouse to the other would have been free. Now you know why Shakespeare said, "Let's kill all the lawyers."

Talk to Him to Save Money

Don't let your divorce sink to the level of the couple I just described. If you and your husband mutually agree to handle this task yourselves, you can divide your property any way you see fit. Although each state has its own laws regarding property division, the laws merely serve as a guideline of what's appropriate. It's really up to you!

Extra Attention Required: If there are significant or complex assets that are tough to value, a lawyer will likely be necessary to present your property division arguments to a judge.

Be proactive during negotiations, keeping communication with your husband open and nonhostile. This is important, because if you can't reach a compromise, then there will be no choice but to involve the court system in this process. (For tips on how to keep negotiations civil, see Chapter 17.)

How to Get the Job Done

Property division involves "dividing" the bank accounts, cars, houses, cash, jewelry, stocks, furniture, and all other marital assets, property, and interests, through a series of offers and counteroffers, until a compromise can be reached. A fair compromise exists when you and your husband feel you both gave up a bit more than you had originally intended, but each can live with the outcome.

When you are ready to begin dividing your property with your spouse, take out your asset inventory checklist prepared as part of your Pre-Divorce Plan. Use the asset checklist to help you keep track of your property as you negotiate, so you don't inadvertently leave out items that you may be entitled to. Don't count on your husband to remind you if you forget to claim a possession that he secretly wants to keep for himself. Since you have already done your homework and know exactly what marital assets are available to you, by hitting every item on the checklist, you ensure that you will not walk away with less than you deserve.

Before you begin discussions, use your asset inventory list as a reference to make two columns on a pad of paper. The first column will include all your "must have" items—in other words, the property you intend to walk away with. This column represents the minimum of what you are willing to accept. The second column will list all the marital property you are willing to let go, or your "don't need" items. These items will serve as your bargaining chips. Since your spouse won't know that they have little value to you, you can offer them to him in exchange for him letting you keep items from your "must have" column.

After preparing your two columns for your own refer-ence, you are ready to begin the negotiation process. Go through your original asset inventory list with your hus-band. Each of you should make give-or-take proposals for each item on the list, until you reach the bottom. Anytime your husband makes a demand for property that appears on your "must have" list, counter his request by offering him items from your "don't need" column, and that column only. There will be cycles of offers, counteroffers, acceptances, and rejections until all the property on your original inventory list has been distributed.

Next, take out your debt inventory list, also prepared as part of your Pre-Divorce Plan, and negotiate who will be responsible for each and every debt. If you owe money on your car loan or have outstanding credit card debt, you may want to negotiate for your spouse to assume responsibility for all or part of your debt. You will also want for him to agree to assume responsibility for any debts he incurred during the marriage, so you will not be held responsible after the divorce.

Once you have reached agreement on all the items, draw up a written property settlement agreement spelling out your decisions. Be sure to sign your names at the bottom. Most states require the signatures to be witnessed and notarized. The final step will be for a judge to approve your property division agreement (by finding it fair to both sides), so it can be deemed legally valid.

A Property Division Success Story

My good friend "Diane" successfully conducted the property division phase of her divorce without attorney intervention. Although she and her husband had "lawyered up," she decided they would work together without legal assistance to split their stuff to save money. Diane told me she got tired of hearing *ka-ching* every time she called her lawyer.

Diane asked her husband to make a list of all their property, and suggested they would rotate picking items off the list to keep. The couple owned and lived in a 650-square-foot apartment in Manhattan. They had stocks, furniture, and a car, and each had a retirement account through their respective employers.

When the husband showed Diane his list, she spotted three particular items that caused her to almost fall off her chair. He wanted to know how they would divide the food in the refrigerator, the alcohol in the liquor cabinet, and the magazines. Yes, you read it right. Her spouse insisted on negotiating over the spices, the condiments, some half-opened bottles of vodka, and back issues of *Vogue* and *Time*, thereby winning him the "Cheapskate Husband of the Year" award. Diane was speechless.

When Diane questioned her husband's practicality, he became belligerent, threatening to call the lawyers if she refused to address his "concerns." Diane knew there was no point in spending four hundred dollars an hour dividing the ketchup. So she gave him exactly what he wanted and focused her energy on dividing valuable assets. Despite having to deal with her husband's pettiness, Diane's commitment to dividing property without attorneys potentially saved her and her soon-to-be-ex thousands of dollars in billable hours.

No More Talking—See You in Court

If divorcing spouses can't agree on a property division, the decision will be made by a judge, usually at a court hearing or trial. In court, each side will try to convince the judge what property exists, how much it's worth, and which spouse should receive it. Evidence may be presented and testimony may be taken at the courthouse. A trial over property division issues can last from several hours to several days.

Results from the courtroom are unpredictable. They can vary depending on your judge, what he or she thinks is fair, and how he or she applies the local law to your case. It's always better to decide yourselves, rather than have a judge who knows little to nothing about you, your marriage, and your lifestyle dictate your financial future. (If trial is unavoidable, Chapter 8 will walk you through the courtroom process each step of the way.)

CHAPTER 16

The Support Report:
How Much Alimony and Child Support Will
Be Coming Your Way

Alimony Basics

Alimony is a support payment made by one spouse to another during or after a divorce. The more modern terms for alimony are *maintenance* or *spousal support*. *Alimony pendente lite* is temporary alimony, usually ordered by a court for the time period a divorce is pending or while a couple is legally separated.

> **A Must:** Even if you do not seek alimony, a smart strategy is to secure *one dollar* in alimony as part of your divorce agreement. In many states, this maneuver preserves your right to receive some form of alimony in the future. Without a token one-dollar alimony award, you may be barred from returning to court to seek spousal support should your financial circumstances change due to illness or loss of a job.

Some wives forgo alimony in exchange for other property. (The reason they do this is explained later in this chapter, in the section entitled "Alimony vs. Uncle Sam.") In many states, you can waive your right to alimony with a written agreement, but I recommend you do *not* do this.

You and your husband can negotiate your own alimony agreement. There are no limitations on the amount of the payments or how long you can receive them. However, alimony agreements are typically structured to end when the recipient remarries.

Deciding the amount of an alimony award is a complicated and stressful process. Wives often complain that their husbands won't give them enough money to maintain their lifestyles. Husbands often gripe that their wives are trying to drain them dry and should get a job to support themselves.

Strategy Tip: Some lawyers will tell wives that they can expect to receive approximately 30 to 40 percent of their husband's income as alimony. In my experience, no practitioner should be giving you a hard-and-fast rule or guaranteed results. Courts decide alimony on a case-by-case basis, and there is no reliable way to predict exactly what you will get. Read ahead to see what factors determine how much you get.

When negotiating alimony, there are no formulas, percentages, or calculations to rely on. Couples usually weigh each other's earning potential against the value of other assets or property each spouse is expected to receive from the divorce. Some factors for you and your spouse to consider are:

- Your monthly living expenses and debts
- Who will reside in the marital residence
- Your liquid finances
- Your income after taxes
- How much of the noncustodial spouse's income goes to child support
- How much each spouse needs to live

If you and your husband can't agree on an amount, court intervention will be necessary. But because judicial decision making is so uncertain, spouses frequently settle alimony disputes between themselves instead of taking their chances with the judge.

What Will a Judge Do?

Judges have enormous discretion in structuring alimony awards, although they are limited by a maximum amount set by law. A court's decision is not subject to any guidelines or special formulas. Maintenance can be awarded to either spouse depending on who the primary breadwinner is, the length of the marriage, the earning capacity of both parties, the ability of the parties to work, and the employment skills and education level of the spouses. Most courts will decide an amount after doing a lifestyle analysis.

A Closer Look at Factors a Court Considers
in Awarding Alimony

The length of the marriage

The longer the marriage, the more support you can get. If a court considers your marriage to be short-term, you may not be awarded any alimony.

Which spouse is the breadwinner

Breadwinners are expected to share their income with the financially weaker spouse.

The education, job skills, and employment histories of the spouses

The court will consider what each spouse is capable of earning in the future based on his or her skills, training, and prior work experience.

A question wives often ask is, *"If I am not working during the marriage, and then get a job while the divorce is pending, will this affect the size of my alimony award?"* The answer to this question is, "It's possible."

This issue poses a big divorce catch-22. If a stay-at-home mom obtains employment while going through a divorce, she may get a lower spousal support award, even if she needs the extra money to pay the bills. That's because she has increased her earning potential.

Don't let the possibility of getting a reduced support payment dissuade you from updating or building job skills. Unless your alimony will run indefinitely, it's better to be employable in the future when support runs out than to have no skills or experience to fall back on.

 **Be Careful:** If you are job hunting, be careful of whose desk your résumé ends up on. Husbands can introduce résumés into evidence in an attempt to pay you less support, by showing the judge you are capable (at least on paper) of earning an income.

The effect of age and health on a spouse's earning ability
If a spouse can't work, the court will factor that into the size of an alimony award.

Contributions to the marriage
If you sacrificed your career by taking a lesser-paying job or worked fewer hours so your husband could succeed in his career, courts may factor that contribution into your alimony.

What other property or assets you will receive from the marriage
If a wife is awarded significant income-producing assets or real estate, the judges may balance the value of that property against the amount of alimony she would receive.

Who the children live with
The spouse who has primary child custody or resides with the

kids may be prevented from entering the workforce and will need spousal support in addition to child support.

Alternative sources of income

If a wife receives a large income from an inheritance, gift, trust, or separate investment, it may affect whether she receives alimony payments or how much she will receive.

Alimony vs. Uncle Sam

In most states, a wife can trade her right to receive alimony for other marital assets or properties. Or she can choose to receive a one-time lump-sum cash payment, known as a *settlement*, in lieu of alimony. There are huge advantages to receiving a one-time payout rather than a monthly or weekly alimony check.

If you accept a cash settlement, you receive that money tax-free. But if you opt for alimony, Uncle Sam gets a portion of your award. Whoever *receives* alimony in a divorce is required to pay income taxes on those payments. Whoever *pays* alimony gets a tax deduction.

The other advantage to receiving a lump-sum payment up front instead of alimony is that your ex can fail to pay alimony on time, pay erratically, or skip payments altogether. This would force you to go back to court after the divorce to battle for his compliance with the support agreement. You also may run the risk that if his financial stability later deteriorates, he can return to court to request a reduction of your payments. Even if you have a previously approved support order, most courts will not compel a husband to continue paying when it is impossible for him to do so. When a husband's financial picture has drastically changed or he is unable to work, the court can order a modification or a suspension of spousal maintenance.

 Bonus Tip: Your ex-husband likely won't win a reduction in his payment requirement if you can show that he intentionally stopped working to avoid support orders.

Sometimes husbands will demand that their wives give up other property in exchange for an immediate lump-sum settlement payment. This may or may not be worth it. Be sure to calculate your strongest financial option before deciding what type of support payment you will receive.

Child Support

Child support or *child maintenance* is a payment for the care and support of children received by the parent who has *physical custody* of them (also known as the parent with whom they reside). Even if a mother and father have *joint custody* (meaning they are equally responsible for making decisions about health, welfare, and education), the spouse who doesn't live with the children and is not their primary caregiver has a legal obligation to pay a proportion of the costs in raising them until age eighteen, nineteen, twenty-one, or twenty-three, depending on the state where the divorce was filed.

If there are children from the marriage, spouses will spend significant time deciding who the kids will live with; who will pay for their health insurance and college education; who will make the decisions regarding their medical needs, education, and religious schooling; and how visitation will be structured for the noncustodial parent. But the issue of child support, including how much must be paid and for how long, is decided *for you* by state law.

Calculating Payments

Child support payments are determined based on official state Child Support Guidelines, which provide percentage formulas that dictate what the payments should be. The calculations often take into account the costs of supporting the child, as well as each parent's financial ability to contribute. Most states have their own Child Support Guidelines worksheets or computer programs, which allow spouses to calculate a dollar amount, often based on a percentage of combined parental income, taxes, insurance costs, how many days the child spends with each parent, and other factors.

Couples can choose to disregard percentage formulas set by state guidelines and enter into their own agreement of what they think is fair. But their agreement will always be subject to court approval, with most judges requiring an acceptable reason for why the arrangement is fair. Any father's decision to pay more than what the state guidelines require will undoubtedly pass muster with the court.

Some states let the parents work out how the payments

will be made. But other states collect child support payment directly from a parent as if it were a tax, and forward it to the child's primary caregiver.

 **Bonus Tip:** If you are the one making child support payments directly to your spouse, pay with money orders or checks. These payment methods offer proof that could come in handy should your spouse later claim that he or she didn't receive the payment.

Child Support Equals Free Money

Unlike alimony, child support payments are tax-free to the recipient and not tax-deductible for the payer. Watch out for husbands who try to avoid taxes by fiddling with the structure of your support agreement. They will attempt to negotiate paying a lower child support amount in exchange for making higher alimony payments. Their true intention is to save money by taking the alimony tax deduction. You will end up paying more in taxes on the larger alimony check, instead of no taxes on a larger child support payment. Should the government catch on that your support agreement is suspect, your husband could get in trouble with the IRS.

When Will I Receive My Payments?

Even if a divorce takes months or years to resolve, a court can enter judgment for child support and custody before the marriage is legally dissolved. A court may order *temporary child support* while the divorce is pending. After a couple resolves their divorce issues, the court can then make the temporary order permanent or modify it based on any new information obtained in the divorce proceedings. A child support order will be incorporated into the final divorce agreement at dissolution.

Child Support Stories of the Rich and Famous

In the brutal New York divorce battle waged between Revlon billionaire Ron Perelman and his ex-wife, socialite Patricia Duff, the amount of child support the mother sought for her daughter, Caleigh, was staggering (initially $1.6 million a year). Ms. Duff submitted an affidavit to the court outlining what her monthly expenses were to maintain Caleigh "in the lifestyle to which she was accustomed." She asked for tens of thousands of dollars per month to cover expenses for Caleigh's birthday parties, nannies, wardrobe, furniture, vacations, pets, and grooming. An interior decorator testified that it would cost one hundred thirty thousand dollars to remodel Caleigh's bedroom. The couple's custody battle lasted twice as long as the marriage, but things did not fare well for Ms. Duff. She eventually lost legal custody. However, she was granted extensive visitation rights.

On the opposite coast, actor Jim Carrey's ex-wife, Melissa, the mother of the couple's daughter, reportedly walked away with a multi-million-dollar divorce settlement. Melissa also made hefty demands for child support payments. She requested more than one hundred thousand dollars to fund a variety of private lessons, a personal trainer, and a Pilates room for their teenage daughter. Because of her husband's vast wealth, few in Hollywood considered these demands extraordinary.

The Secret Truth Behind "Spending" Child Support Money

There's a big secret concerning how child support payments are spent—one that most custodial parents don't discuss in public. When support payments are high, there may be extra money left over after the children's expenses are paid. Some ex-wives secretly spend that money on themselves or use it to supplement their alimony payments.

Clearly a mother is not allowed to indulge herself at the expense of her kids. But in most states, if there's child support money left over after child-rearing costs are paid, wives don't have to account for how the remaining cash is spent. That's because courts believe that money used to make the mother's life more comfortable also benefits the kids. For example, if the mother installs a hot tub in the yard and the kids use it, they are gaining a lifestyle advantage from their child support payments.

However, some states, like Colorado, Delaware, Florida, Indiana, Louisiana, Missouri, Nebraska, Oklahoma, Oregon, Washington, and sometimes Alabama, will demand a periodic accounting from the custodial parent on how child support "income" is spent.

Be Careful: Women everywhere, be on the lookout! When fathers begin to scrutinize a mother's spending habits after a divorce and don't like what they see, they may deploy a sneaky tactic. I have seen examples where men whose ex-wives appeared to supplement their lifestyles with leftover child support money invent a reason to drag these women back to court to battle for a change in custody. The fathers' secret agenda? To lower their child support obligation.

Deadbeat Dads

While child support laws vary from state to state, all noncustodial parents must pay according to the child support court
order or they will face legal consequences. Some judges will
garnish wages or tax refunds, suspend drivers' or professional
licenses, or prosecute the delinquent parent. If a garnishment
isn't possible, sometimes courts will order a bench warrant
to haul a deadbeat parent back to court, or even impose jail
time. But to force a deadbeat dad to pay, he must be physically
located within the state where the support order was issued.

My friend Laurence ("Larry") Greenberg, a top New York City
divorce attorney, represented a wife whose husband, a wealthy
oncologist, fled the state owing three hundred thousand dollars in
back child support. Because the doctor left the jurisdiction, Larry
could not find him to enforce collection of the money.

But Larry came up with a brilliant plan. He relentlessly
searched for the doctor's name on the Internet over several months.
One day he struck gold. The deadbeat dad was scheduled to be
the star guest lecturer in New York City at a conference of the
country's most prestigious cancer doctors. On that day, Larry set
a trap. Knowing there was an outstanding warrant for the doctor's
arrest, he advised the sheriff's office of the date, time, and place
where the doctor was scheduled to appear when he arrived back
in New York City.

On the date in question, when the famous MD was called up
to the stage to begin his medical lecture, the sheriff was waiting in
the auditorium. Law enforcement agents met up with the doctor

at his seat and handcuffed the gentleman in front of his colleagues. Before the doctor could even make his opening remarks, he was hauled away and escorted to a prison cell downtown. The man who had taken a Hippocratic oath to serve others had to serve time in the city jail until he paid off his child support obligation.

How Legal Separation Affects Alimony and Child Support

A legal separation—unlike an informal separation, where the couple chooses to live apart without a valid separation agreement or court order (discussed in Chapter 5)—gives spouses the legal right to enforce obligations upon each other, such as child support or the payment of temporary maintenance and spousal support, also called *alimony pendente lite*. A separation that is not legally sanctioned does not provide for court-ordered remedies, but has a different advantage: Any alimony-type support payments you receive without a written agreement in effect are not taxed as income, because legally the marriage is considered to be intact.

Once you have addressed final alimony and child support/ child custody issues, it's time to breathe easier. You have just decided two out of the three major divorce issues (if relevant to your case) that require a resolution in order for a divorce to be granted—property division being the third. You are another step closer to signing off on a final divorce agreement. The end of your marriage is in sight.

CHAPTER 17

Cashing Out: How to Negotiate Like a Pro

Strike a deal with your husband by learning the art of divorce negotiation. My top five negotiation techniques will help you to be assertive, hold your ground, outsmart your spouse, and get what you want at the bargaining table. The best time to use the techniques is *before* you file the divorce papers or immediately after your divorce begins, when your relationship with your husband should still be relatively amicable.

A smart and less expensive way to achieve a property settlement agreement is to work directly with your spouse and decide on maintenance and asset division in a nonconfrontational manner. Negotiating your own divorce will not only save money on lawyers' fees, but also quite possibly get you better results. (Yes, I was a divorce attorney, and yes, I just said that.)

But bear in mind that there is a trade-off for not using lawyers to negotiate if your husband becomes belligerent or your discussions otherwise break down. You place yourself directly in the line of fire, without an intermediary to deflect his anger or hostility. Bearing the brunt of a heated verbal assault or intimidation tactics is emotionally draining and can wear you down. I will show you how to defuse a contentious situation. But if dealing face-to-face with your husband is too stressful or he is too volatile, it's best to have an attorney intervene.

Holding Your Ground

To effectively negotiate your divorce, it is important to listen to your spouse, hear him out, then state your position. If your husband attacks, take a deep breath and remain coolheaded. If necessary, count to ten, and move past any personal jabs or insults. Don't respond to them or sink to his level. Remain composed and keep talking. (For more tips on how to keep your emotions in check during a divorce, see Chapter 9.)

Another tactic is to turn on the tears and make yourself appear vulnerable to soften any of his aggressive advances. Even if he is putting you through hell, remember that now is your sole opportunity to get what you need before going your separate way. By staying calm, you can stay the course and make a deal.

Don't Be a Doormat

Your goal is to leave the marriage financially self-sufficient. Don't bargain away your rights and entitlements for the future by letting him wear you down in the present. No one should be bullied into walking away without securing a fair share of the marital assets. Tackle the negotiation phase of your divorce by learning the art of divorce negotiation.

Have Your Cake and Eat His, Too: Winning Negotiation Strategies

Here are the inside tactics and techniques I developed as a lawyer, which I also used to negotiate my own divorce settlement. My negotiation strategies can be applied not only to divorce, but to any aspect of your life where you want to reach a successful compromise.

Negotiation Technique #1: Greed Is Good

First Principle: Always ask for more than you really want, but within reason, so you don't destroy your credibility.

Second Principle: Never take his initial offer in the first round of negotiations.

Third Principle: Start your numbers off high and end up somewhere in the middle.

Greed Is Good in Action

Let us say your marital property inventory list consists of:

- a house
- furniture
- a valuable sculpture

- two cars
- a stock portfolio
- his retirement plan

You intend to walk away from the table with:

- half the proceeds from the sale of the house
- one of the cars
- half the stock portfolio

Begin negotiating by asking for more than you really want, but within reason, so you don't destroy your credibility. For example, ask for:

- half the house
- the sculpture
- a car
- the whole stock portfolio
- half his retirement plan

Greed Is Good Recap

By demanding extra property, you have now created bargaining chips. If your husband rejects your initial demand and counteroffers with less, you will appear to be "meeting him in the middle" by backing away from some of the additional items you didn't want in the first place, and accepting what appears to him as a little less.

So, for example, let us say he counteroffers with half the

sale of the house, a car, and none of the stock portfolio or retirement plan (what we lawyers call a lowball offer). You can then respond, "I will let you keep your retirement plan intact in exchange for half the stock portfolio." If he rejects your new offer, wait for his next move and continue to modify your demands by offering to give up your "do not want" items until you reach your bottom line.

Bargaining is a psychological chess game. By initially asking for more than you want and subsequently appearing willing to accept his lower counteroffers, you can convince him that he's getting a good deal. This will encourage him to compromise.

Negotiation Technique #2: Kill Your Spouse with Kindness
First Principle: Sugar works better than vinegar.

Second Principle: Dialogue with your spouse in a neutral, nonaccusatory tone of voice.

Third Principle: Bite your tongue and refrain from any negative or hurtful comments.

Kill Him with Kindness in Action

You: The condo has appreciated by a hundred and fifty thousand dollars. If you want to keep it, you could buy me out for seventy-five thousand dollars.

Him: You know I don't have that kind of money. You are

being totally unrealistic, selfish, and ridiculous.
You: You may be right. Maybe I am being unrealistic.
But I thought that would be a fair way to do
things. Maybe you could liquidate some of
your investments to come up with the cash
if you don't have it. Or do you have another
suggestion?

In this example, the technique has you "agreeing" with him, rather than counterattacking him. Even if you know your calculation of the amount necessary to equally divide the condo is realistic and fair, by being agreeable instead of defensive, you are encouraging him to keep the dialogue going.

If you treat your husband respectfully during the negotiation process (even if you don't respect him), your positive behavior will yield productive interactions. If you don't treat him respectfully, don't expect your negotiations to go far. What man would want to make a deal with a hostile, hateful woman? Keep your personal feelings to yourself during this phase of the divorce using the techniques in Chapter 9. Husbands are more willing to compromise when they feel appreciated and respected.

****

Take It from Someone Who Knows: Calm and rational dialogue during negotiation really works. At one point during my property division negotiations, my husband balked when I asked him to give me a very valuable antique Persian rug from our living room. We had purchased it at auction during an intense bidding war. He was adamant about keeping it, and threatened to walk from the negotiating table if he didn't get his way. I kept the dialogue from stalling by gently reminding my husband of these three points:

1. Lawyers get paid by the hour to divide property.
2. If we can't accomplish this between ourselves, we will have to hire professionals to sort out our private lives.
3. Why risk delaying our divorce and spending all our money on attorneys?

While I did eventually capitulate the rug, I got him to agree to purchase me new living room furniture in exchange—all because I kept the conversation flowing by appearing to be friendly, cooperative, and reasonable.

****

What If Being Nice Doesn't Work?

Of course, some spouses will be impossible to deal with from the onset. They may refuse to take your calls or continually make unreasonable and unworkable demands, destroying any realistic opportunity to negotiate face-to-face. If your spouse is belligerent and won't meet you halfway, it's time to move the negotiation phase of your divorce from your living room to the courthouse to duke it out in front of a judge.

Negotiation Technique #3: The Pseudo Yes

First Principle: In divorce, a *yes* won't stick unless it's in writing. *Yes* him to death in the initial negotiation.

Second Principle: Hit him with *no* when you get closer to sealing the deal.

Third Principle: Suggest the possibility of an amicable resolution, but in reality promise nothing.

The Pseudo Yes in Action

Him: I want the condo.
You: That's a possibility, we can talk about it.

This response appears to leave the door open for your consideration of his proposal down the road. But appearances are deceiving, and later, when the issue resurfaces, you will get back to him with a *no*.

Him: I want to keep both cars.
You: Maybe. We'll see.

Maybe is a frequently used form of *pseudo yes* that lets the opposing party believe that a *yes* is a possibility. You can later change your *maybe* to a *no*.

Him: I want you to split your 401(k) with me.

You: I would have to run that by my attorney/my
mother/my priest/my accountant/my therapist
before I can commit to you.

After initially appearing to consider his request, you will come back to your husband with a *no* later in the negotiations. You can explain the reason for the *no* by stating that you consulted with [the designated person], and they are preventing you from agreeing to the request. (For example, "I spoke to my accountant, and he said I can't transfer my stock dividends to you.")

Because you have put the responsibility or blame for your response on an outside party, it's harder for your husband to get angry with you when you subsequently turn him down.

Him: I want alimony.
You: I will look into it/I will think about it and get
back to you.

This response also appears to keep open the possibility of a *yes*. But after you "look into it" and get back to him, you will need to explain that unfortunately, his proposal is unworkable.

Him: I want to sell the vacation home.
You: Probably/Possibly that could happen.

Probably, like *possibly*, puts off a debate for a future date. Hopefully, by the time you get to the discussion down the road, you can distract your husband by raising other issues.

The *Pseudo Yes* Recap

The theory is that at the initiation of negotiations, it is better to appear agreeable, even if you don't plan on delivering. There will be times when you and your spouse want the same thing, and one person will eventually need to capitulate. To win a compromise, keep your opponent in the negotiation long enough to sway his opinion or change his mind by employing the *pseudo yes* technique.

As you can see, the technique works by using ambiguous language that implies you *may* grant your husband's requests— no matter how absurd—but that doesn't actually commit you to following through. Anything said in a divorce negotiation can be changed at any time before the parties sign on the dotted line. Only a signed written contract is enforceable.

The goal is to continue with a back-and-forth negotiation. Since you have kept communication going, you can now start to employ additional negotiation techniques from this chapter to improve your chance of success.

Why it works: By passing the responsibility for the stalemate to another party, you keep the dialogue open, and your husband can't blame you for not delivering. Now is your chance to renew negotiations on disputed issues and get him to back down. By modifying your *pseudo yes* to a *no* when it comes time to finalize the agreement, you can redirect the conversation and force your opponent to re-examine his position.

Changing Your *Pseudo Yes* to a *No*

When you come back to the negotiating table for a final round, it will be time to change your previously uttered *pseudo yes* to a *no*. Here are some ways to gracefully accomplish this.

You say: "My accountant/financial adviser/rabbi/ priest/lawyer won't let me sign the divorce agreement if it states you get the condo because that would violate my right to an equitable distribution. What else can we negotiate to balance things out so we can go ahead with an agreement?"

The Best Defense Is a Good Offense

I am not recommending that you make false promises. I am merely suggesting that you leave open the possibility that you *might* meet his demands, by using ambiguous language. Your husband is an adult, and adults know that a promise of a possibility does not always yield a result.

Negotiation Technique #4: The Marlon Brando Technique

First Principle: Fake it until you make it.

Second Principle: Don't reveal your hand.

Third Principle: To alleviate friction from the opposing side, orchestrate your compromises.

The Marlon Brando Technique in Action

We start with the scenario that you and your spouse own a condo together. It has appreciated dramatically over the past few years. You alone have done substantial decorating and supervised the improvements. You have no intention of giving it up in the divorce, but your spouse seems to want it too.

Here's how the dialogue might flow if you didn't use the Marlon Brando Technique:

> *Him: I want the condo.*
> *You: No way. I decorated it. I found it. I want it. My*
> *sister lives around the corner. You should find a*
> *new place.*

Because you showed him that the condo matters to you, you just gave away your hand in the first round. Now your husband will have a bargaining chip. He may believe that if he drives a hard bargain with the condo, he'll get you to make bigger concessions and give up additional marital assets as you try to hold on. Or, now that he knows what you want, he might not back down just to be vindictive.

Here's your response using the Marlon Brando Technique:

> *You: I am not that attached to the condo, but I really*
> *don't want to uproot our child and have to move*

her in the middle of the school year. Would you
consider letting me keep the condo in exchange
for me giving up a claim to your retirement
benefits?

The key to success is to put on your poker face and act disinterested. Otherwise your husband will gain leverage over you when you tell him exactly what's on your agenda. Act as if the condo is not a big concern. Continue to negotiate over it, but don't allow him to think losing it is the end of world for you. Keep talking, making proposals, and applying the other techniques in this chapter to maneuver his interest away from the condo and toward other property.

Have You Ever Noticed?

Have you ever noticed that when someone else wants something that you have, it suddenly seems more desirable? It's called "The more you want it, the more I want it" syndrome. This very syndrome often takes hold of parties involved in divorce negotiations. If your husband thinks you want something very badly, he may fight harder to keep it for himself, even if he doesn't want it in the first place. So when something important to you is on the negotiating table, apply the Marlon Brando Technique and act like you just don't care. By keeping your composure and a steady voice when you bargain, you avoid raising his suspicions that the item has value to you, and you stand a better chance at getting what you want.

Negotiation Technique #5: Repeat, Repeat, Repeat!
First Principle: Repeat.

Second Principle: Repeat.

Third Principle: Repeat.

Repeat, Repeat, Repeat in action

You: Will you let me keep the station wagon? I need
the car to get to work.
Him: You have been a real bitch the past few weeks.
Why should I listen to anything you have to say?

His reply is clearly not responsive to the question asked!
When the response does not match, repeat the question or
statement and wait for a different answer. For as long as he
will stay in the conversation, calmly repeat yourself as many
times as necessary, until he has nothing left to say or do but
answer your question. This method requires patience on your
part and the ability to bite your tongue until you get a desired
result.

You repeat: Dan, will you consider letting me keep the
station wagon?
He says: Go to hell.
You repeat: I would really like to try to work this out

> *between us. Will you consider letting me have the*
> *station wagon? I need a car to get to work.*

Eventually he should respond to the question at hand because he will run out of nonresponsive answers.

The theory behind the technique's success is that when you repeat something over and over, it eventually sticks. First the listener runs out of time and energy to continue diverting your attention away from the issue at hand. Finally there will be nothing left for him to say but the actual answer to the question.

Why Divorce Negotiations Require
Implementing Tough Tactics

Some might argue that my negotiation methods are politically incorrect, because at times I encourage you to manipulate your spouse. But divorce is an artificial situation requiring artificial behavior. Once the legal system inserts itself into the family unit, married partners become legal adversaries. The deception I am talking about in this chapter does not involve cheating your husband out of his entitlements or acting unethically. Rather, I encourage you to propose a fictitious agenda to prevent your spouse from learning your true intentions.

It happens all the time in corporate boardrooms across the country. And it works well in divorce. If your spouse doesn't know your bottom line, he has less of an opportunity to back you into a corner. He will then be more likely to bargain with you intellectually rather than emotionally, or out of spite or vengeance. That's a strategic way to bolster your bargaining position.

Your Negotiation End Results

Once negotiations are complete, you and your spouse should draft a final divorce contract, also known as a *settlement agreement* or a *dissolution agreement*, designating which spouse gets which marital asset and who pays alimony and/or child support. In most states, all you need to do is list the agreement reached for each item you negotiated in its own separate paragraph, but check with your state's rules on how the agreement should be structured.

Be Careful: It is possible during the emotional turmoil of divorce negotiations, specifically do-it-yourself negotiations, for domestic violence to rear its head, even if it has not done so during the marriage. Be prepared that your spouse may express his unhappiness over the divorce by responding to your negotiation attempts with hostility. If he exhibits extreme or escalating anger, physical violence, or threats of violence, leave the negotiating table at once and terminate direct contact. If you sense at any time that you are in potential danger, follow your instincts and seek professional help.

Sample Settlement Agreement

Plaintiff v. Defendant
Bishop County Family Court
Docket No. FA345

The plaintiff wife and the defendant
husband in the above-docketed matter
hereby agree to settle their divorce
action in the following manner:

1. The house at 23 Maple Street
will go to the wife.
2. The furniture and china set will
go to the husband.
3. The husband will pay the wife
alimony in the amount of $500 per
month.
4. The husband will keep the 1999
Acura automobile and the wife will
keep the 2003 Buick automobile.
5. The husband will pay monthly
child support pursuant to the state
Child Support Guidelines.
6. The wife will have primary
custody of the minor children, and
the husband will have visitation on
weekends.
7. The wife will take both tax
deductions for the two minor children
for the next IRS calendar year.

8. The husband will maintain the wife and children on their current health insurance policy under his employer, General Electric, for the next six years. The husband will pay all premiums, as well as copayments for the children. If the husband changes his employment or is no longer employed at General Electric for any reason, the husband will pay for a comparable health insurance policy for the wife and children during the designated time period.

_____ _____

Jane Doe   John Doe
Dated:

Once everything is set in writing, both spouses will sign at the bottom, the same way a business contract is executed. Most divorce agreements need to be witnessed by one or more individuals when signed, as well as notarized, depending on your state's requirements.

CHAPTER 18

Seven Things to Do Before
You Sign Your Divorce Papers

Throughout this book we have planned and strategized steps to take before and during the divorce. Once you are near the end, it's time to plan for your life after divorce.

Before you sign on the dotted line of your divorce agreement, there are several items that should not be overlooked. Be smart about protecting your future financial stability and preserving your lifestyle. Prior to finalizing your divorce contract, cover your bases by following this essential to-do list.

The "Don't Forget to Do This Before You Divorce" List

1. Secure Health Care Coverage

With health insurance premiums soaring at several hundred dollars a month per person, securing future coverage before you finalize your divorce proceedings is crucial. Regardless of whether your husband is self-employed, self-insured, retired, or unemployed, the one thing you don't want to forgo in a divorce is paid health insurance benefits. Don't leave your marriage without getting a written guarantee from your spouse that he will provide health insurance benefits for you (and your children), especially if he is the primary breadwinner.

Bonus Tip: In some divorces, I have seen husbands stop paying their wives' health insurance bills or remove their wives' names from their policy entirely, jeopardizing continued coverage. To ensure your husband's efforts at maintaining your coverage post-divorce, demand that he send you proof of premium payments after they are made.

If possible, have your husband give written consent to pay for health insurance for a set number of years, or at least until you obtain employment that offers you coverage. If you currently receive coverage from his employer, make sure he agrees in writing to continue paying the premiums after the divorce, so as not to interfere with your continued coverage.

It is also wise to add a special provision to your divorce agreement that he maintain you on the same "quality and quantity of coverage" that you had while married, regardless of whether he changes jobs or health insurance carriers in the future. Even if you have your own coverage now, ask him to agree to provide health-care benefits if your circumstances change.

Be Careful: If you are currently insured through your husband's employer, once the marriage is legally dissolved, you may be prevented from continuing as an insured family member on his policy. However, you will be protected under a federal law called COBRA (the Consolidated Omnibus Budget Reconciliation Act). This law requires that insurance companies continue coverage for a former spouse of an employee, as long as that spouse was already covered prior to divorce. Under COBRA, you may stay on your spouse's employee health insurance policy for up to three years after a divorce, *as long as you notify his employer within sixty days after your divorce becomes final that you intend to continue coverage.*

Don't rely on your spouse to give his employer notice on this critical issue. Send written notice yourself to avoid jeopardizing your coverage.

2. Get a Written Decision on Who Is Responsible for Debt and Tax Liabilities

A husband and wife may be equally liable for certain types of debt accrued during the marriage, even after the divorce is granted. Although a debt incurred before the marriage is usually the responsibility of the person who assumed it, it's still possible for both spouses to be held responsible, especially when one spouse cosigned a loan for the other.

Bonus Tip: Take your name off the mortgage. If your husband is awarded the family home or any other real estate where he will be the sole owner, remove your name from any mortgages or property loans that you have co-signed. If you don't, you will be responsible for future payments or the balance of the loan should your husband default. Most mortgage companies and banks will require you and your spouse to refinance the mortgage in order to remove one party's name from the loan.

Processing fees can range from several hundred to a few thousand dollars to prepare a new mortgage document. Be sure to add an extra provision to your divorce agreement requiring your husband to pay any fees that may be incurred.

To protect yourself from future debt liability or a ruined credit rating, it's crucial to tackle debt issues before your divorce agreement is finalized. Do not leave your marriage without a written assignment of responsibility for debt and other financial obligations. The last thing you want a year down the road is for your ex-husband's creditors to be knocking at your door for you to pay his outstanding bills.

If your husband borrowed money to build a business or took out student loans while married, it may be considered marital debt that both spouses are required to repay, even if you didn't cosign the loan. Creditors can also hold you liable for marital debts, even if your husband is the only one to possess the item that resulted in the debt after you part ways. Your divorce agreement should address who will pay which creditor and how much.

In addition, both spouses are also equally liable for any taxes owed as a result of filing a joint return. Decide which one of you is going to be responsible for paying any tax bills that may arrive after the divorce is final.

> **Bonus Tip:** If your husband is obligated to pay outstanding debt, whether it's marital or premarital debt, be sure your divorce agreement has a provision where he will "hold you harmless" from liability after the divorce is finalized. This way, you may be protected if his creditors, who are not bound by your divorce agreement, look to you for repayment after the marriage has been terminated.

3. Remove His Name as a Beneficiary on Your Life Insurance Policy, Financial Accounts, and Last Will and Testament

Make sure to protect your family's financial future by removing your husband's name as beneficiary from any life insurance policies, your last will and testament, or any financial or brokerage accounts. Even after the marriage has been terminated, your ex-husband can end up inheriting your estate or the proceeds from your life insurance policy that you intended to leave to your kids or other family members if he is still listed as a beneficiary. Change all your accounts to reflect that he will not receive benefits in the event of your death.

4. Get Life Insurance for Your Husband If He Will Be Paying You Support or Maintenance

If you are planning on receiving alimony and child support from your ex, it's a good idea to negotiate for a life insurance policy for your husband where you and the children are his beneficiaries. Life insurance is a form of divorce insurance. It will protect you after divorce by providing a guaranteed income in the event of his death, when you would no longer receive support payments. This is an especially good planning device for stay-at-home moms, or women with little income of their own, who rely almost entirely on post-divorce maintenance and support.

5. Seek Disability Insurance

A working wife who earns less than her husband may want to have her spouse purchase a disability insurance policy for her. That way, if she becomes sick or disabled and can't work after the marriage is dissolved, she will have insurance coverage to make up for her lost wages. This is particularly useful to women in poor or declining health or whose job stability is uncertain.

Bonus Tip: If you already have your own coverage, you can also negotiate for a clause in your divorce agreement stating that if you lose your employment due to circumstances beyond your control (ill health, layoffs, or firing), your husband will make increased alimony payments.

6. Decide Who Will Claim Income Tax Deductions

Don't forget to address which spouse will claim any available tax deductions. Couples should decide who will be entitled to take the year-end tax deduction for interest payments on a mortgage or business loan, and who will claim the kids on their tax return. (After a divorce only one parent can take a tax deduction for each child.) Tax deductions can result in a refund of several thousand dollars to the spouse who claims them.

7. Get at Least One Dollar in Alimony

Here is an important reminder from Chapter 16. If you have agreed to a lump-sum settlement in lieu of monthly alimony payments or have waived alimony, make sure to get a written statement in your divorce agreement awarding you "one dollar" in alimony. In most states, this token alimony award preserves your future right to request alimony should there be a change in your financial circumstances after the divorce.

No Need to Worry

If you do not accomplish some of the items on this list, that's okay. Your family financial situation, for example, may not allow for the purchase of a disability insurance or life insurance policy. Weigh your priorities and determine which items are most important for your future financial stability, and don't sign the divorce papers until you are satisfied you have achieved what you need. In my experience, the two most important items a wife should have in place before divorcing is health insurance coverage and one dollar in alimony if she has waived her right to spousal support. By following the "Don't Forget to Do This Before You Divorce" list, you will be in a secure position to close the final chapter of your marriage. You are now ready for the court to grant your dissolution.

CHAPTER 19

Case Closed: What to Expect When the Marriage Is Officially Over

When my ex-husband and I attended our final dissolution hearing, the whole "day in court" took less than an hour. As the plaintiff, I was required to take the witness stand in the courtroom and swear under oath that the marriage was irretrievably broken, all the issues were resolved and agreed to in writing, and that both parties wanted the court to grant the divorce. I must admit, that part was a little unnerving—even for me, a lawyer who appears in court on a daily basis. In the witness box, I felt like a spotlight was shining on me, making me feel a bit self-conscious and vulnerable.

But when I was on the stand, looking out into the courtroom and down at my husband seated at the defendant's table, it was the first time that I actually felt that I was involved in a lawsuit. Since we'd handled all of the divorce on our own, this was the first time our case brought us into a courtroom. The reality that the State of Connecticut was about to officially terminate my marriage had finally set in. (For those of you involved in a contested divorce, you will see the inside of a courtroom much earlier and more often than I did.)

After the judge reviewed our signed divorce agreement and financial affidavits, he banged on his gavel and loudly stated, "Granted." It was finally over.

Some Final Things to Do and Not to Do After the Divorce

Once your marriage is officially over, there are a few items that will need your attention. The hard work is behind you. But here are some final things for you to do—and not to do—to keep your post-divorce life running smoothly.

1. Take your name off any rental leases, joint charge accounts with merchants, and utility bills

There are probably a few remaining open accounts where your name is listed jointly with your ex-husband's that might have been overlooked up until this point, like the electric bill or a joint line of credit. Or, you may have forgotten to revoke documents that were co-signed during the marriage and continue to be legally enforceable, such as a rental lease. If so, you could be exposed to financial liability for any default in payment or outstanding bills incurred by your ex after the divorce until the time you remove your name.

If your former spouse remains in a rental property that served as your marital residence, remove your name from the lease. If you maintained joint charge accounts with merchants or qualified for a joint line of credit during your marriage, close them. If accounts with utilities, telephone or cell phone companies, or service providers remain open for your ex's continued use, take your name off the accounts. Send certified letters to landlords, lenders, and service providers that you are no longer responsible for payments because the marriage has been dissolved, and/or you no longer own or reside at the residence. Keep a copy of the letters for yourself.

2. Keep a "child custody log"

If you are a parent, child custody issues may continue to surface post-divorce until the time your children reach adulthood. Either parent can return to court at any time after the marriage is terminated, claiming a change in circumstances and requesting a modification of custody, child support, and visitation. If you believe your ex is not satisfied with the existing arrangements, protect yourself from his future attempts to change the status quo by keeping an ongoing "child custody log." To make a record, document anything unusual you observe or hear from your children about your ex-husband or their experiences during visitation with him. Particularly note if your child suffers emotional problems after spending time with your ex-spouse. Collecting evidence is the best way to protect your family and arm yourself for any future family court action.

3. Avoid maligning, bad-mouthing, or gossiping about your ex

Disparaging your ex in public can come back to haunt you. Refrain from damaging his reputation after the divorce and keep your dirty laundry private. Down the road you may need something from him, or need him to agree to modify the divorce contract, or grant you some flexibility with its terms. You may need him to take the kids during "your time" so you can go on vacation. You may need him to forward important mail addressed to you that he received by mistake. If he learns you are bad-mouthing him, forget about solving simple post-divorce issues with a phone call or e-mail.

He can refuse to deal with you and force you back to divorce court for trivial requests or easily resolved matters. Further damage can be done to an existing relationship between cooperating parents. If you trash the reputation of your children's father, you will likely jeopardize any rapport between you. When two divorced parents can no longer remain civil, psychologists warn that the fallout can have a long-term adverse impact on the children.

****

Take It from Someone Who Knows: Malicious gossip and innuendo from one former spouse about another surfaced within my own circle of friends and added more fuel to the fire of an already bitter divorce. When I introduced two of my married girlfriends to each other, they made plans to get together for lunch and decided to make some matches among the singles in our neighborhood. They compared lists of all their single friends, both male and female, to see whom they could introduce and set up on dates. During the conversation, one friend mentioned an eligible ex-husband who was back on the market. When she described him, she repeated his claim that he was previously married to a "horrible woman" who had "mental issues." That woman turned out to be the best friend of the second matchmaker.

No one says you need to like your ex-spouse, but preserve his reputation the same way you would expect him to preserve yours. It's now time for both of you to heal, not to inflict additional pain. If you are having trouble managing your anger, which is understandable following the difficult experience you just had, it may be time to seek professional help.

****

What to Expect After Your Divorce Is Final

Once your divorce is final, you may find that the dissolution of your marriage is affecting you in unexpected ways. Divorce is a life-altering experience. Even if you feel psychologically prepared for the single life, the realization that your identity has changed from married woman to divorcée can still be unsettling. Many wives who thought they had moved on experience profound emotional reactions immediately following their divorce. Prepare for the possibility that your initial post-divorce experience may be a difficult and sad time for you, even if up until this time, it's all you had been waiting for.

After splitting up, you may find yourself distracted or floundering until you get your bearings. There will likely be shifts in your financial status, ties with friends (especially those who took your spouse's side), and standard of living. But always keep in mind that the fallout from divorce is temporary, and as time passes, your life will naturally get itself back on track.

Coping with the Emotional Aftereffects of Divorce

Your relationship with your former spouse wasn't built in a day, so you should certainly give yourself sufficient time to mourn its undoing. But there is an "emotional deadline" following divorce, when it comes time to stop living in the past or reliving the end. Most mental health professionals will say a year to two should be sufficient time to heal. Any longer than that becomes unhealthy for thoughts of the marriage breakdown to continue to rent space in your head.

Mourning the loss of your marriage past a reasonable grieving period becomes problematic when your mental state begins to adversely affect your personality, health, or emotional stability. If your divorce leads to depression, mood disorders, or anxiety attacks, and/or you are still suffering after a reasonable amount of time has passed, you are probably past your emotional deadline. It is time to seek professional help.

You probably don't need to worry about occasional instances of minor emotional discomfort. There's nothing unusual about experiencing uneasiness or anxiety when you run into your ex, his friends, or a member of his family. It's natural to feel your heart beat faster when you pass a restaurant where you celebrated your anniversary, recognize the same type of car your ex used to drive on the street, or spot an item that reminds you of him. But if your focus on the divorce becomes an obsession, or you are dwelling for months on end, it's time to take proactive steps to move on.

Getting Over It

Even though I wanted my marriage to end, I still felt post-divorce anxiety about whether my new life would be satisfying, whether I would meet someone new, and whether the decisions I made during the divorce would get me where I wanted to go. Then I realized that it was time for me to follow the same advice I had given my clients and friends.

There are two important factors in getting over a divorce. The first is: *Don't second-guess your divorce decisions!*

Asking yourself questions like, "Did I get enough money?" "Should I have fought harder?" "Should I have demanded the house?" and "Was my financial settlement package too small?" is counterproductive to moving on with your life. Nor is there any way to tell after the fact whether you could have changed the divorce dynamic by acting, feeling, or behaving differently. You can't predict what kind of decision or judgment call would have affected your future. Live with the decisions you made. Things worked out the way they are now, because they were "meant to be."

The second most important factor in getting over a divorce is: *Don't second-guess your decision to divorce.*

You divorced for a reason. The marriage wasn't working. That does not make you a failure. In fact, these days being divorced often has more cachet than being "single and never married," especially in the dating world. Think of your former union as a useful life experience that has prepared you for your next relationship. After all, failed first marriages are great practice for successful second marriages. And for every door that closes, another one eventually opens.

Letting Go

Give yourself some time and distance from the divorce to gain perspective. Time really does heal wounds. It's unrealistic to work on getting over your relationship at the same time you are immersed in a legal battle. Now that you have completed the process, let some time pass for you to emotionally deal with this significant event in your life.

After the dust has settled is usually when you get the clearest picture of the dynamics of your former marriage and the reality of just who it was you were married to. With this clarity comes understanding and peace of mind. When you realize your past relationship no longer has an influence on your present state of mind, it's easier to let go.

My close friend experienced a startling post-divorce "surprise" that revealed the true extent of her ex-husband's pettiness and insensitivity. Because some time had passed since the divorce, she was able to process the event calmly and rationally.

When she dropped her son off for weekend visitation with his father, she saw random memories of her marriage scattered across her ex-husband's lawn. He was holding a garage sale and dumping her former possessions, which he had either refused or "neglected" to return during the divorce and which had caused her significant heartache. Her Tiffany cake plate, which he vigorously fought to keep with the assistance of a high-priced attorney—yes, a cake plate—was sitting on the lawn with a price tag of fifty cents. Her old clothing, which she left in the closet after leaving the house when the divorce began, was on sale for three dollars an item. And her pregnancy books were available to expectant mothers at the bargain price of one dollar a piece.

The irony of this experience is that it made my friend realize that there was light at the end of the divorce tunnel, and she had reached it! Whereas during her divorce she would have been reduced to tears by the same situation, her subdued reaction and lack of anger toward her ex confirmed for her that she had truly succeeded in letting go of the past and moving on.

When the right amount of time has passed after your divorce, it will also happen for you. A new life is just around the corner. You are ready, prepared, and on your way!

Afterword

I hope reading this book has given you the knowledge and confidence you need for a successful and dignified divorce. While I no longer handle divorce cases in my current law practice, I will always remain a member of "The Divorce Club." It is a club with millions of members from coast to coast. It is a sisterhood made up of those of us who have gone through this experience and come out the other side—a little wiser, a little tougher, certainly more practical, and definitely stronger.

I don't regret being in this club, because it made me who I am today. My former marriage and my divorce still influence how I choose to lead my life and with whom I choose to take the journey. You, too, will be blessed with the positive things that come from your divorce, whether it's your children, the comfort and support of your family, or the opportunity for personal growth. I wish you all the best on the start of your new life. *Welcome to the club.*

Glossary

alimony monetary support payment made by one spouse to another during or after a divorce (also called *maintenance* or *spousal support*)

alimony pendente lite temporary alimony awarded by a court while a divorce is pending or while a couple is legally separated

allegation an unproven statement of fact contained in a divorce complaint

answer a written response to the allegations in a divorce complaint

asset item of ownership, usually having exchange value or convertible into cash

child support guideline   state guideline that provides percentage formulas dictating the amount child support payments should be

child support   payment for the care and support of children received by the parent who has physical custody of them (also called *child maintenance*)

community property   any property acquired or income earned during a marriage by the labor of either party, excluding separate property, such as inheritances, gifts from third parties, and most personal injury awards

community property state   a state in which each spouse is entitled to a one-half share of community property

contested divorce   a divorce that is challenged due to the couple's not being able to agree on all the issues, such as alimony, property division, child support, or custody

credible   the legal term for *believable*

defendant   the spouse who is served with divorce papers (also called *respondent*)

deposition   an out-of-court examination of a witness where oral testimony is taken under oath

dissolution hearing   a court hearing at which spouses ask a judge to approve a signed divorce agreement and grant a divorce (also called *termination hearing* or *final hearing*)

divorce agreement   a binding legal document outlining everything a couple agrees upon in contemplation of ending their marriage

divorce complaint   a legal document filed with the court to initiate a divorce action and request a dissolution of marriage (sometimes called an *information* or a *petition*)

divorce decree   a formal court order granting a divorce

equitable distribution state   a state where marital property is divided based on what's "fair and equitable"

fault divorce   a divorce where one spouse is required to make a legal accusation of fault against the other as to why the marriage failed

financial affidavit   a sworn financial statement indicating the assets, property, expenses, and debts of each spouse individually (also called *disclosure of assets statement* or *net worth statement*)

forensic accountant an accountant specialist who investigates financial and business-related issues, usually used in or suitable for courts

grounds legal reasons why a marriage should be terminated

hearing a court proceeding before a judge that deals with individual divorce issues instead of the whole case

interrogatories sets of written questions that are posed to an opposing party in order to gather factual information during a lawsuit

irretrievably broken a divorce catchphrase for a marriage that is damaged beyond repair

legal discovery process a legal procedure that allows each side of a divorce lawsuit to gather information about the other

marital property any property accumulated from the date of the marriage until a divorce action is commenced, excluding inheritances, gifts from third parties, and most personal injury awards

motion a formal written request for court action on a case (also called an *application*, an *order to show cause*, or a *request for a court order*)

no-fault divorce a divorce where no legal accusation of blame is placed and neither party is considered at fault for the marriage breakdown

order a court directive that must be followed by the party/parties to whom it is directed in a lawsuit

perjury the act of lying under oath

physical evidence evidence that is tangible and can be touched or viewed

physical custody a parent's right to have the child/children live with him or her (also called *primary custody*)

plaintiff the person who initiates the divorce lawsuit (also called *petitioner*)

prenuptial agreement a written agreement entered into by a couple in contemplation of marriage, which provides in advance for some or all of the terms of a future divorce

qualified domestic relations order (QDRO) a court order governing how money will be withdrawn during a divorce from a retirement plan, IRA or 401(k)

request for production a formal written demand that requires a party to produce documents for the benefit of the opposing party (also called *requests for information* or *document demands*)

restraining order a court order that directs one party to avoid contact with another (also called *protective order* or *order of protection*)

retainer an up-front legal fee collected by a lawyer before work begins

ruling a decision made by a judge

separation property any property acquired or owned before marriage; inherited property; property received as a gift from a third party; or property acquired after date of legal separation or divorce, depending on state law

separation contract a document that details the conditions of a formal legal separation

service of process   the procedure by which a summons is served on a defendant (or respondent) when a divorce case is initiated

settlement agreement   a final divorce contract designating the terms both parties have agreed to in order to end the marriage, including who gets which marital asset and who pays alimony and/or child support (also called *dissolution agreement*)

summons   a legal document "summoning" a defendant either to make a personal appearance in divorce court or to respond to the allegations in a divorce complaint

testimonial evidence   oral, written, or recorded statements made by a witness that are relevant to the issues in a case

third-party witness   a witness other than the plaintiff or defendant

trial   the legal procedure by which evidence is presented to a judge in order to get a ruling on the issue in question

uncontested divorce   a divorce that is not challenged by either party

Acknowledgments

To Larry Greenberg, a caring, kind-hearted, generous, and exceptional human being. It is a privilege to call you my friend.

To Cara Bedick, my editor, for her tireless hard work, commitment, and dedication to this book.

To Nancy Grace, for helping me get started on my path as an author.

To Donald Trump, for giving me the incredible opportunity to appear on *The Apprentice* and for "firing" me so quickly, which afforded me a hiatus from my law practice and the time to write this book.

To Wendy Samuelson, for graciously giving her time and advice.

About the Author

Scott Duncan/Duncan Films

Stacy Schneider, Esq., is a trial attorney and former divorce lawyer. She appears regularly as a legal commentator on CNN, Fox News, and Court TV. Ms. Schneider battled in the boardroom with Donald Trump on *The Apprentice* in 2006. She is admitted to practice law in New York; California; Connecticut; Florida; and Washington, D.C. For more information, visit HeHadItComingBook.com.